Cover art courtesy of Serino Coyne

ISBN 978-1-5400-0523-6

7777 W. BLUEMOUND RD. P.O. BOX 13819 MILWAUKEE, WI 53213

In Australia Contact:
Hal Leonard Australia Pty. Ltd.
4 Lentara Court
Cheltenham, Victoria, 3192 Australia
Email: ausadmin@halleonard.com.au

Visit Hal Leonard Online at
www.halleonard.com

Anybody Have a Map?

Music and Lyrics by Benj Pasek and Justin Paul

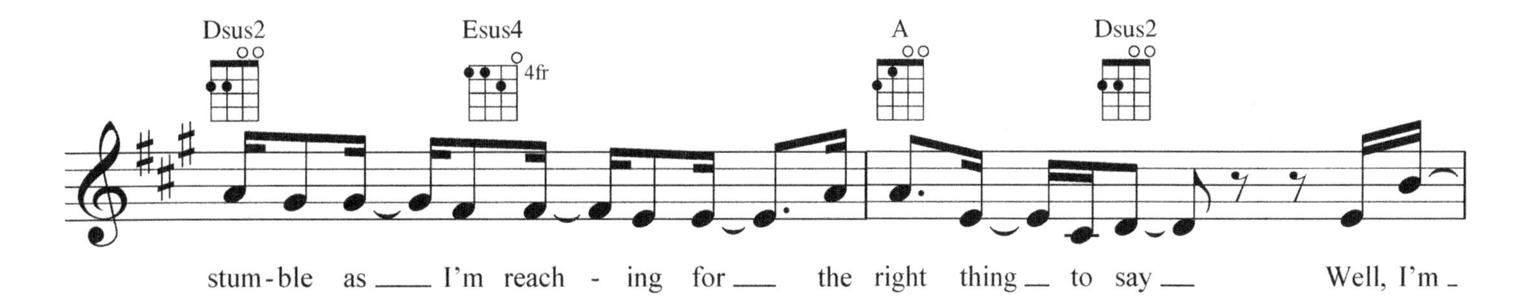
Dsus2
Esus4
4fr
A
Dsus2
stum-ble as I'm reach - ing for the right thing to say Well, I'm

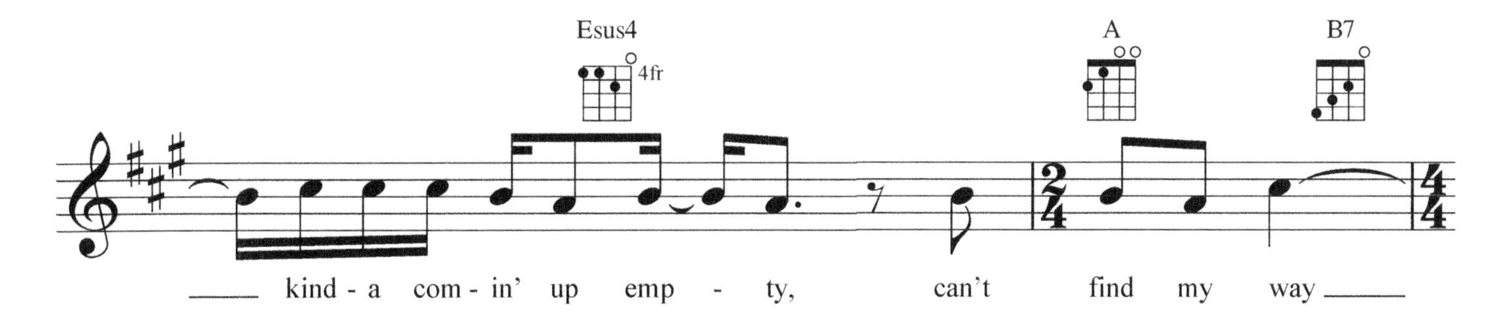
Esus4
4fr
A
B7
kind-a com-in' up emp - ty, can't find my way

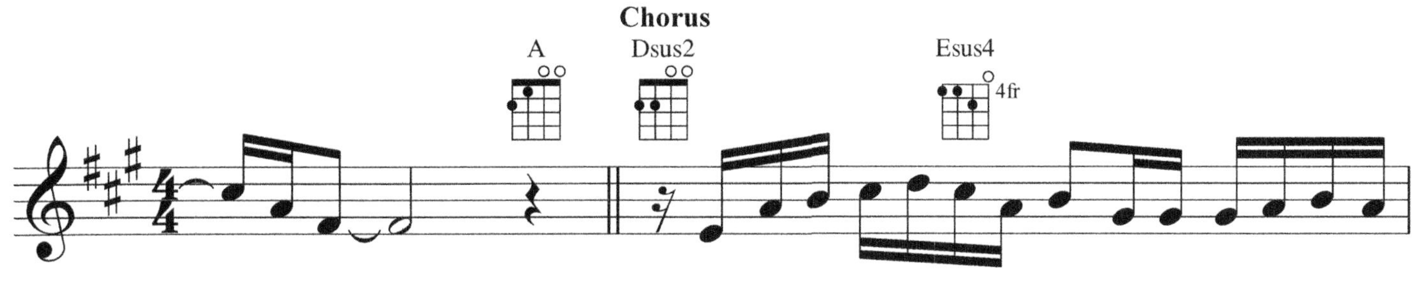
Chorus
A
Dsus2
Esus4
4fr
to you Does an-y-bod-y have a map? An-y-bod-y may-be

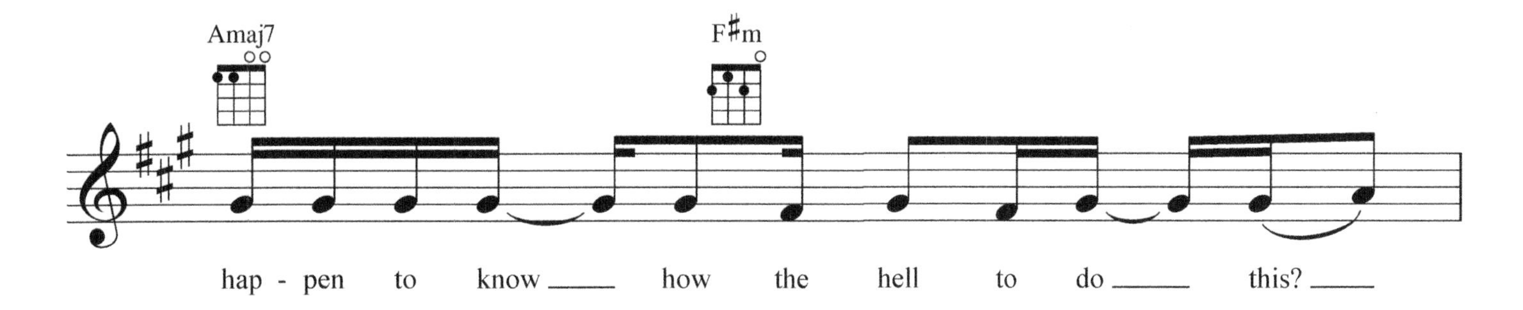
Amaj7
F♯m
hap - pen to know how the hell to do this?

Dsus2
Esus4
4fr
A
I dun-no if you can tell but this is me just pre-tend - ing to know

Dsus2
Esus4
4fr
A
Dsus2
So where's the map? I need a clue 'Cause the scar - y truth is

Bm7
Dmaj7
I'm fly - in' blind and I'm mak - ing this up as I go
A
B♭
CYNTHIA:
3. An - oth - er
Verse
E♭
F
B♭
mas - ter - ful at - tempt ends with dis - as - ter Pour an -
E♭
F
B♭
E♭
oth - er cup of cof - fee and watch it all crash and burn It's a
B♭
F
Gm7
puz - zle, it's a maze I try to steer through it a mil - lion ways But
Cm7
E♭
B♭
each day's an - oth - er wrong turn

Chorus
E♭
F
HEIDI:
An - y - bod - y have a map or
CYNTHIA:
Does an - y - bod - y have a map? An - y - bod - y may - be
B♭maj7
Gm7
hap - pen to know how the hell to do this?
hap - pen to know how the hell to do this?
E♭
F
B♭
I dun - no if you can tell but this is me just pre - tend - ing to know
I dun - no if you can tell but this is me just pre - tend - ing to know
E♭
F
B♭
E♭
So where's the map? 'Cause the scar - y truth is
I need a clue 'Cause the scar - y truth is

Cm7
B♭
I'm fly - in' blind I'm fly - in'
I'm fly - in' blind I'm fly - in' blind
E♭
F
I'm fly - in' blind and I'm mak - ing this up as I go
I'm fly - in' blind and I'm mak - ing this up as I go
Outro
B♭
C7
E♭
As I go
As I go
B♭
C7
E♭
B♭

Waving Through a Window

Music and Lyrics by Benj Pasek and Justin Paul

Pre-Chorus
D
Am7
Em7
D
G
Step out, step out - ta the sun if you keep
C
Am7
get - tin' burned
Step out, step
Em7
D
G
C
D
out - ta the sun be - cause you've learned, be - cause you've learned
Chorus
Em7
C
On the out - side al - ways look - in' in Will I
G
D
Em7
C
ev - er be more than I've al - ways been? 'Cause I'm tap - tap - tap - pin' on the
G
D
Em7
glass Wav - ing through a win - dow I

C
G
D
try to speak but no-bod-y can hear So I wait a-round for an an-
Em7
C
- swer to ap-pear while I'm watch - watch - watch-in' peo-ple pass
G
D
B7
Em7
C
Wav - ing through a win - dow Oh Can
To Coda 1
To Coda 2
G
D
an-y - bod - y see? Is an-y-bod-y wav - ing
C
G
Dsus4
C
G
Dsus4
back at me?
Verse
G
C
D
2. We start with stars in our eyes

G C D G C D
We start be-liev-in' that we be - long
But ev-'ry sun does-n't rise
G C Em D Am7
And no one tells you where you went wrong
Pre-Chorus
Em7 D G C
Step out, step out-ta the sun if you keep get-tin' burned
Am7 Em7 D G
Step out, step out-ta the sun be-cause
D.S. al Coda 1
C D Em7
you've learned, be-cause you've learned.
Coda 1
Bridge
D G C Dsus4
wav - ing When you're fall-in' in a for-est and there's

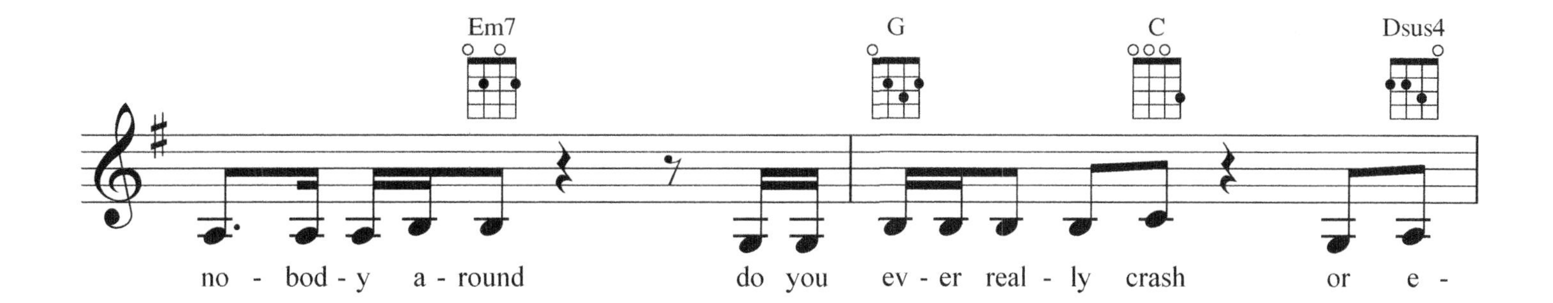
Em7 G C Dsus4
no - bod - y a - round do you ev - er real - ly crash or e -

Em7 G C Dsus4
ven make a sound? When you're fall - in' in a for - est and there's

Em7 G C Dsus4
no - bod - y a - round do you ev - er real - ly crash or e -

Em7 G C Dsus4
ven make a sound? When you're fall - in' in a for - est and there's

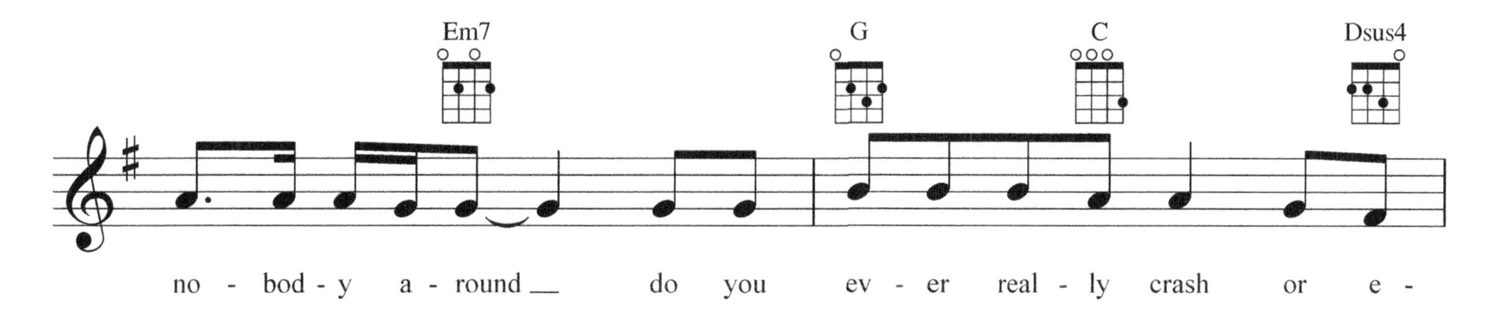
Em7 G C Dsus4
no - bod - y a - round do you ev - er real - ly crash or e -

Em7 G C Dsus4
ven make a sound? When you're fall - in' in a for - est and there's

Em7 G C Dsus4 Em7
no - bod - y a - round Do you ev - er real - ly crash or e - ven make a sound? Did I
G C Dsus4 Em7
e - ven make a sound? Did I e - ven make a sound? It's like I
D.S. al Coda 2
G C Dsus4 N.C. Em7
nev - er made a sound Will I ev - er make a sound?
Coda 2
D
Outro
G C Dsus4
wav - ing back at me?
G C Dsus4 Em7 Dsus4 Csus2
3fr
Is an - y - bod - y wav - ing? Wav - ing Wav - ing
N.C. G
Whoa whoa

For Forever

Music and Lyrics by Benj Pasek and Justin Paul

B♭maj7
F
Tell - ing jokes no one un - der - stands ex - cept us two And we

Dm
B♭
C
talk and take in the view

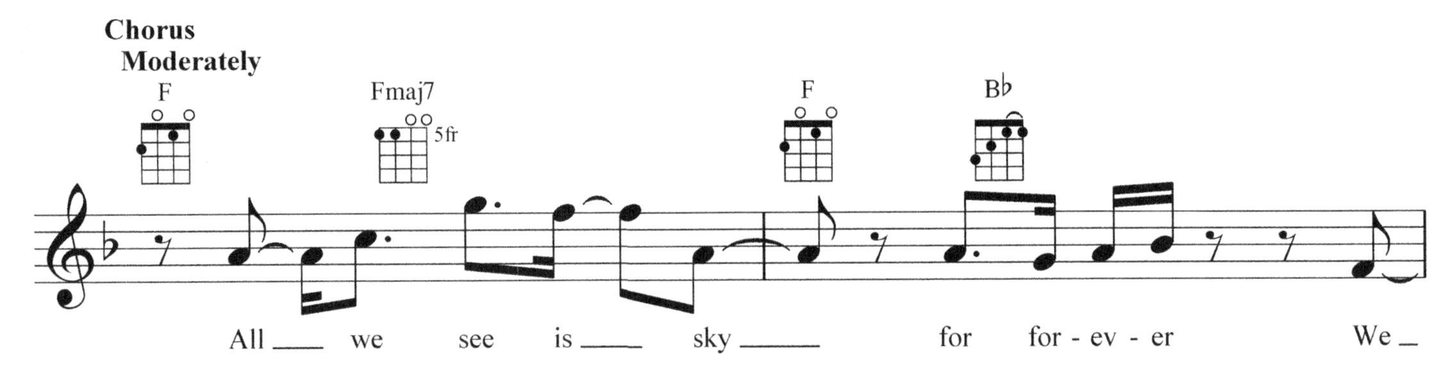
Chorus
Moderately
F
Fmaj7
5fr
F
B♭
All we see is sky for for - ev - er We

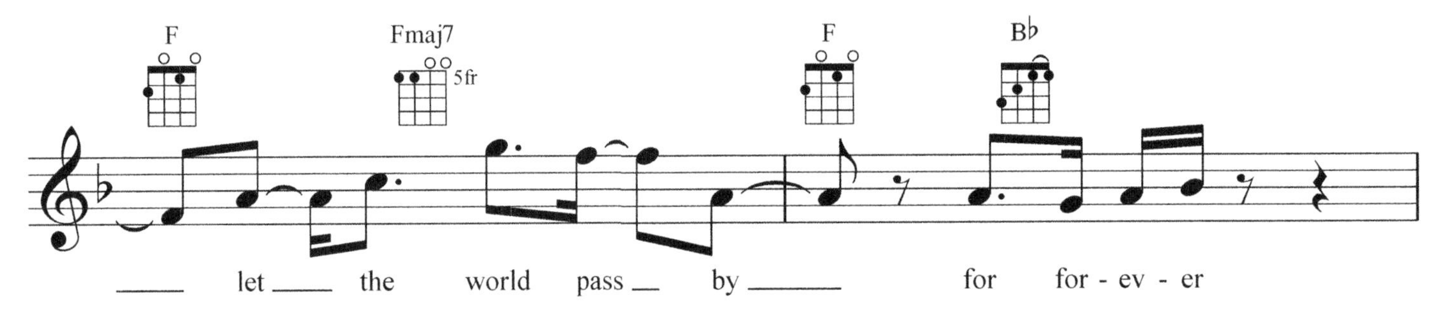
F
Fmaj7
5fr
F
B♭
let the world pass by for for - ev - er

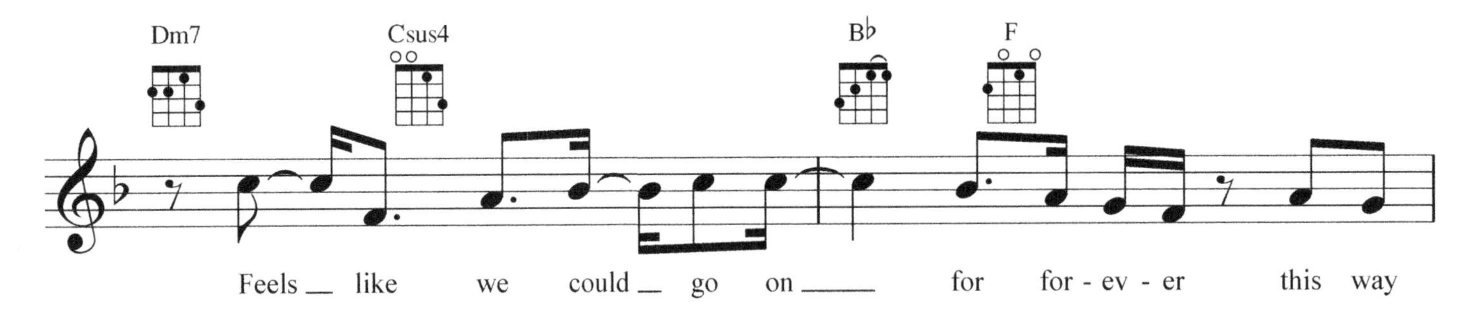
Dm7
Csus4
B♭
F
Feels like we could go on for for - ev - er this way

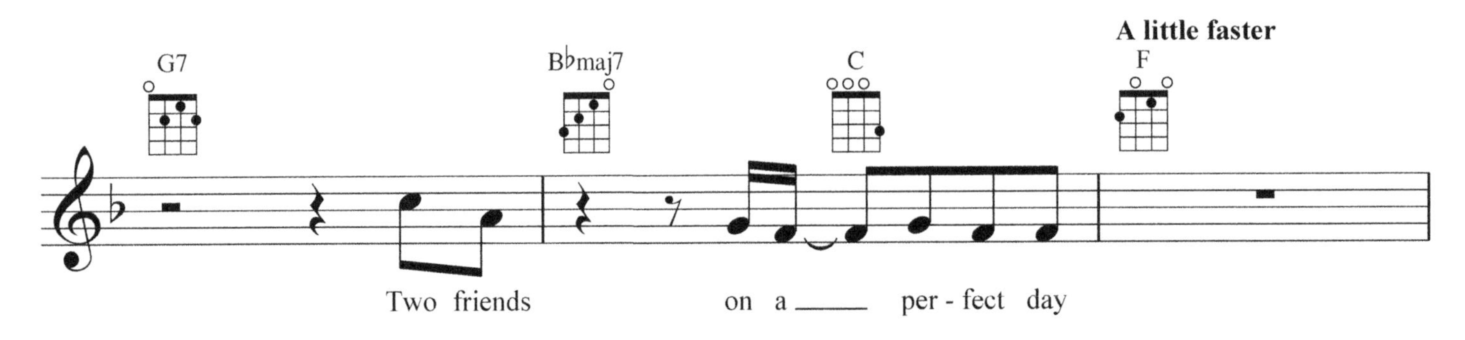
A little faster
G7
B♭maj7
C
F
Two friends on a per - fect day

Fmaj7
B♭maj7
C7sus4
5fr
2. We
Verse
F
Fmaj7
walk a while and talk a - bout the things we'll do when we get out of
B♭maj7
F
school
Bike the Ap - pa - la - chian Trail, or
Fmaj7
B♭maj7
write a book, or learn to sail Would - n't that be cool? There's
B♭
noth - ing that we can't dis - cuss Like, girls we wish would no - tice us but
F
B♭
nev - er do
He looks a - round and says to me "There's

F
no - where else I'd rath - er be" And I say "Me too" And we talk
Dm
B♭
C
Dm
B♭
and take in the view We just talk and take in
Chorus
C
F
Fmaj7
5fr
F
B♭
the view All we see is sky for for - ev - er We
F
Fmaj7
5fr
F
B♭
Dm7
Csus4
let the world pass by for for - ev - er Feels like we could go on
B♭
F
E♭maj7
3fr
B♭maj7
for for - ev - er this way this way
F
Fmaj7
5fr
F
B♭
F
Fmaj7
5fr
All we see is light for for - ev - er 'Cause the sun shines bright

F
B♭
Dm7
Csus4
B♭
F
for for-ev-er Like we'll be al-right for for-ev-er this way
G7
B♭maj7
C
F
Two friends on a per-fect day And
Bridge
Faster
D♭
A♭
3fr
Fm
E♭
there he goes, rac-in' toward the tall-est tree From
D♭
A♭
3fr
Fm
E♭
far a-cross a yel-low field I hear him call-in' "Fol-low me!"
B♭
Gm7
F
There we go won-der-in' how the world might look from up so high
Picking up speed
E♭
One foot af-ter the oth-er One branch then to an-oth-er

F
I climb high - er and high - er I climb 'til the en - tire
Gm Eb F Eb
sun shines on my face And I
Gm F Bb Eb
sud - den - ly feel the branch give way I'm on the ground
Slower
Bb Dm Gm Bb
My arm goes numb I look a - round and I see him
C7sus4 Eb
come to get me He's come to get me And ev - 'ry - thing's o - kay
Chorus
In time, slowly
F G Gmaj7 G C
All we see is sky for for - ev - er We

Picking up
G Gmaj7 G C Em7 Gmaj7
let the world pass by for for-ev-er Bud-dy, you and I
C G Fmaj7 5fr Cmaj7
for for-ev-er this way this way
A tempo
G Gmaj7 G C G Gmaj7
All we see is light 'Cause the sun burns
G C Em7 Gmaj7 C G
bright We could be al - right for for-ev-er this way
A7 Am7 Cmaj7 D7sus4
Two friends True friends on a per-fect
Outro
In time, slowly
G Gmaj7 Cmaj7 D7sus4 G
rall.
day

Sincerely, Me

Music and Lyrics by Benj Pasek and Justin Paul

(in the clear)
EVAN: Why would you write that?
JARED: I'm just trying to tell the truth.
EVAN: This needs to be perfect. These emails have to prove that we were actually friends. Just...I'll do it.
(GO ON)
A7
B7
Verse
Em
G7sus4
C
CONNOR:
2. I got - ta tell you, life with - out you has been hard
G
C
B7
JARED:
C:
J:
Hard? Has been bad Bad? Has been rough Kink - y!
CONNOR:
And I miss talk - ing a - bout life and oth - er
D7sus4
JARED: Very specific.
EVAN: Shut up.
stuff I like my
JARED: Who says that?
par - ents– I love my par - ents but each day's

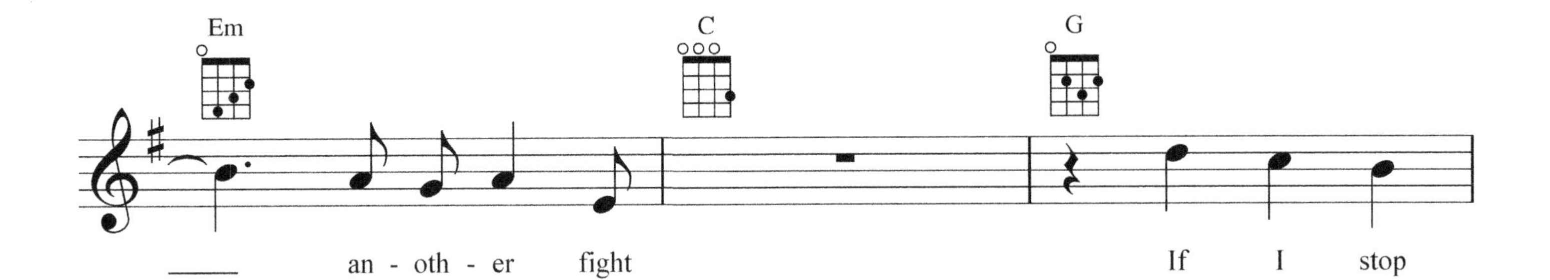
Em
C
G
an - oth - er fight
If I stop

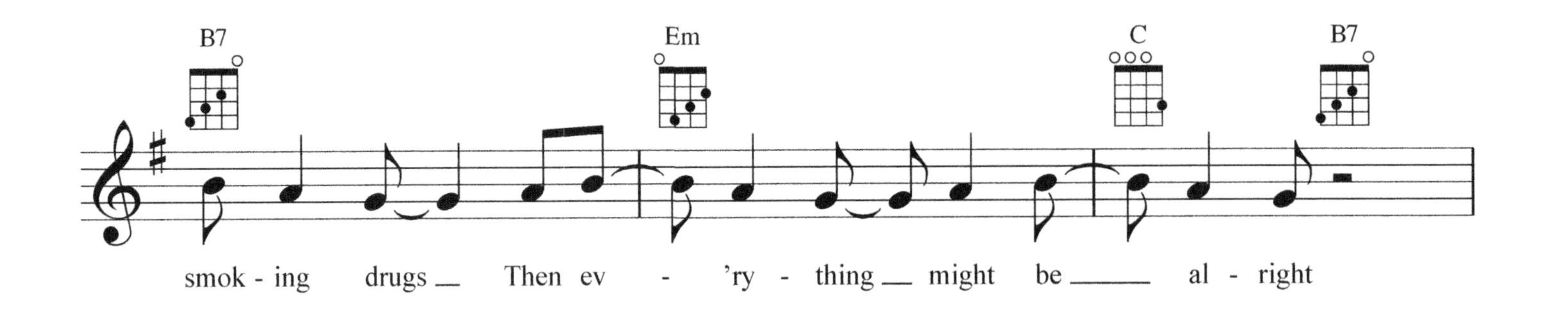
B7
Em
C
B7
smok - ing drugs Then ev - 'ry - thing might be al - right

D7sus4
G
JARED: Smoking drugs?
EVAN: Just fix it.
CONNOR:
If I stop

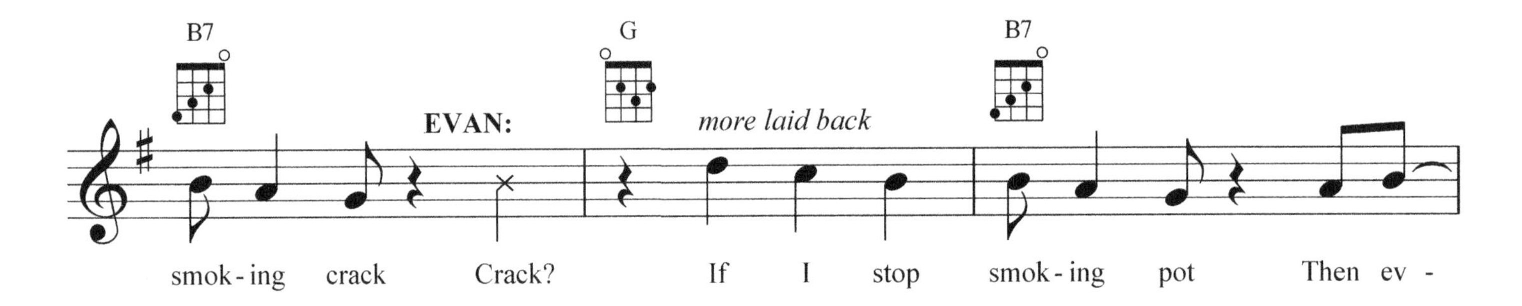
B7
G
B7
EVAN:
more laid back
smok - ing crack Crack? If I stop smok - ing pot Then ev -

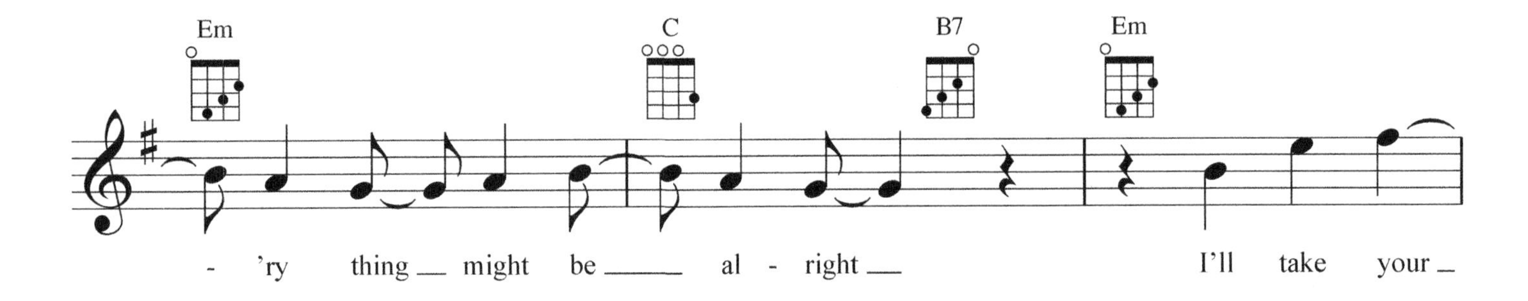
Em
C
B7
Em
- 'ry thing might be al - right I'll take your

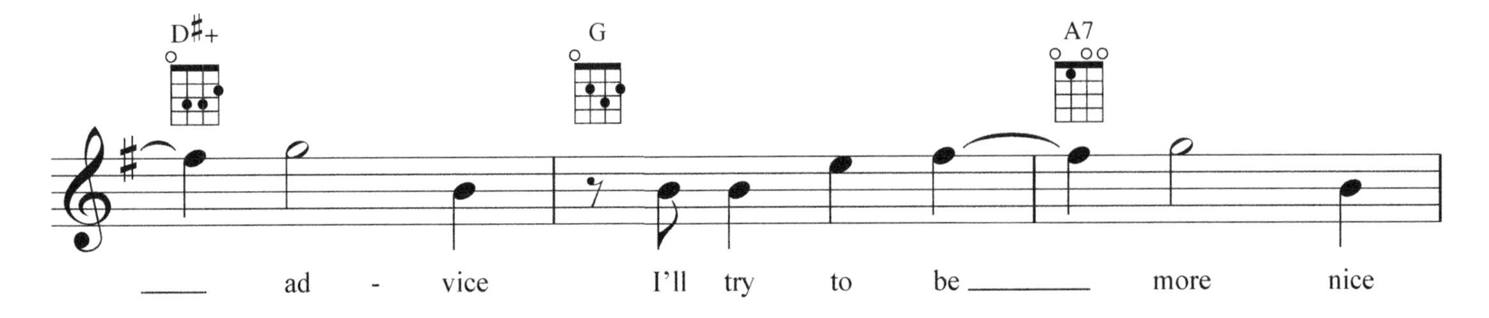
D♯+
G
A7
ad - vice I'll try to be more nice

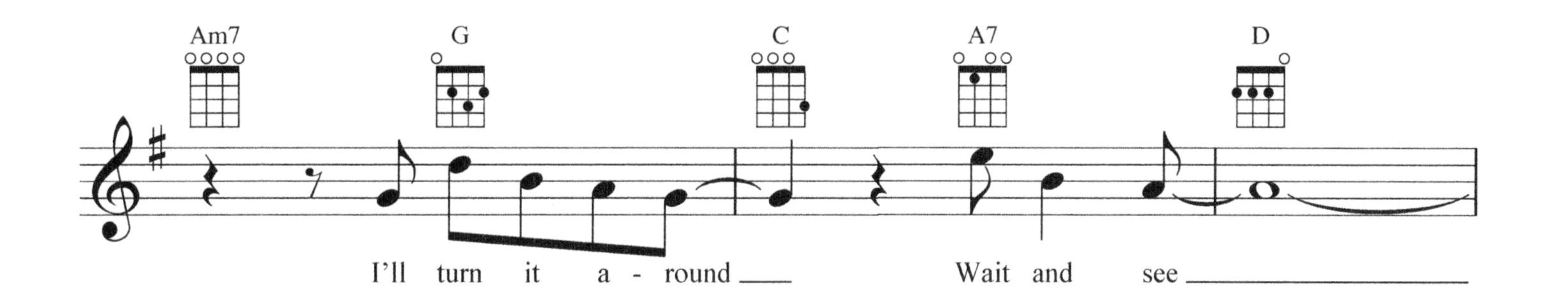
Am7
G
C
A7
D
I'll turn it a - round
Wait and see

Chorus
F
C
'Cause all that it takes
is a lit - tle

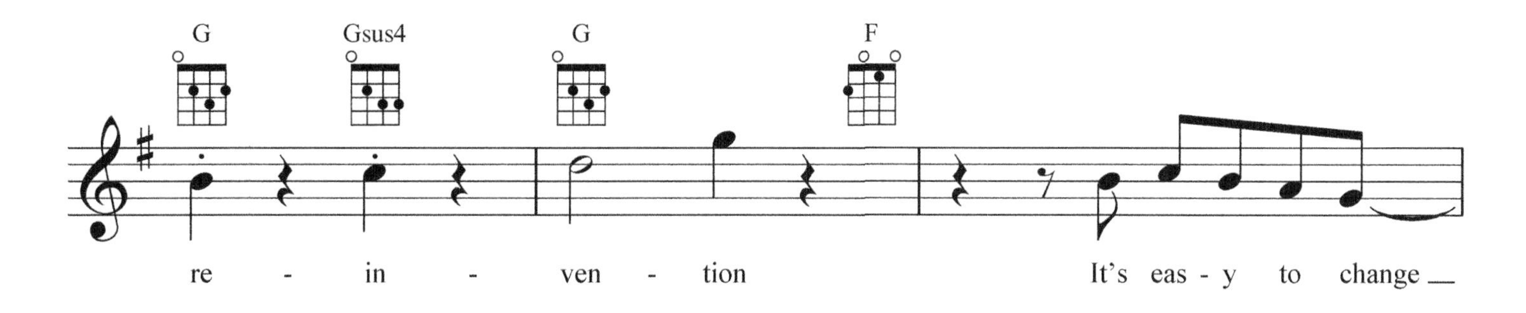
G
Gsus4
G
F
re - in - ven - tion
It's eas - y to change

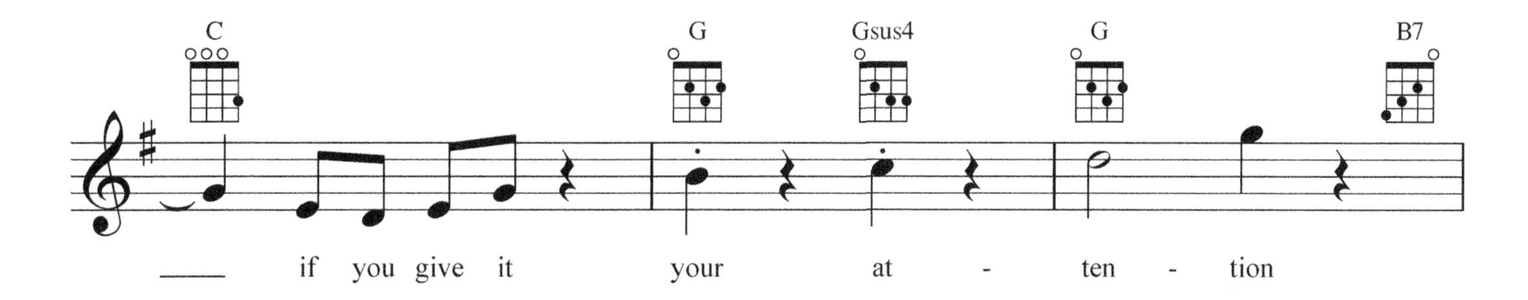
C
G
Gsus4
G
B7
if you give it
your at - ten - tion

Em
D
D7
All you got - ta do
Is just be - lieve
you can be who

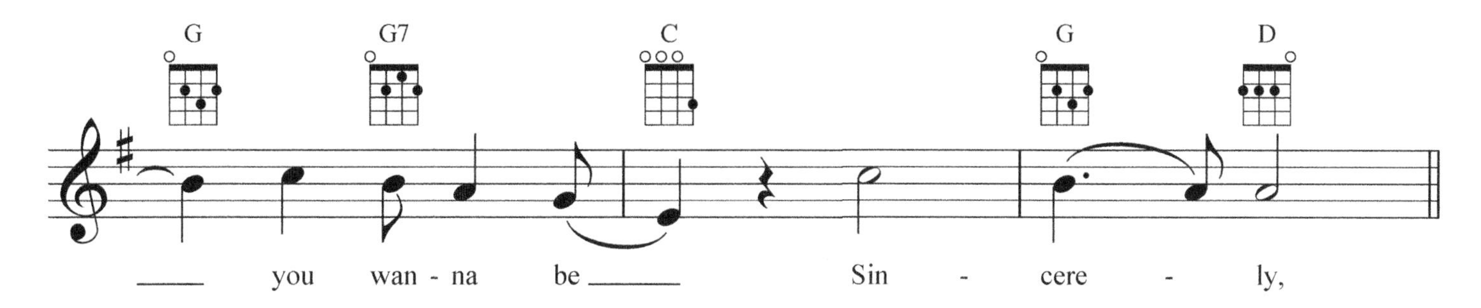
G
G7
C
G
D
you wan - na be
Sin - cere - ly,

Interlude
JARED: Are we done yet?
EVAN: I can't just give them one email...
EVAN: ...I want to show that
G G7 Em G+ G G7
Me
I was, like, a good friend, you know?
JARED: Oh my God...
G6 G+ G G7 G6 G+
Verse
G B7 Em
EVAN:
3. Dear Con - nor Mur - phy: Yes, I al - so miss our talks
C7 G B7 Em
Stop do - ing drugs Just try to take deep breaths and
C B7 Em G7sus4
JARED: No...
EVAN:
go on walks I'm send - ing pic - tures of the most
C G B7 Em G7sus4
JARED: No...
EVAN:
a - maz - ing trees You'll be ob - sessed with all my

C A7 B7 Em
JARED: Absolutely not. EVAN:
for - est ex - per - tise Dude, I'm proud
D#+ G A7 Am7 G
of you Just keep push - ing through You're turn-ing a - round
C A7 D F
I can see
CONNOR:
Just wait and see

Chorus
C G Gsus4 G F
EVAN
CONNOR:
'Cause all that it takes is a lit-tle re - in - ven - tion

C G Gsus4
It's eas - y to change if you give it your at -

G B7 Em
ten - tion All you got - ta do Is just be - lieve
D D7 G G7 C G D
you can be who you wan - na be Sin - cere - ly,
Verse
G Bb
EVAN:
(to JARED)
CONNOR:
Me What the hell? 4. Dear Ev - an Han -
CONNOR:
JARED:
Me My sis - ter's hot. My bad.
D Gm Eb Bb
EVAN:
- sen: Thanks for ev - 'ry note you send Dear Con - nor Mur -
D7 Gm Gm7 C
- phy: I'm just glad to be your friend

Bridge
C7 F F7 D7
EVAN
CONNOR:
Our friend - ship goes be - yond Your av - 'rage
Gm C C7 F F7 D7
EVAN:
CONNOR:
kind of bond But not be - cause we're gay No, not be -
Gm F B♭sus4 B♭
EVAN
CONNOR:
cause we're gay We're close but not that way The
A♭ 3fr E♭ F N.C.
CONNOR:
on - ly man That I love Is my dad Well, an - y -
F G7
EVAN:
You're get - ting bet - ter ev - 'ry day
CONNOR:
way I'm get - ting bet - ter ev - 'ry day

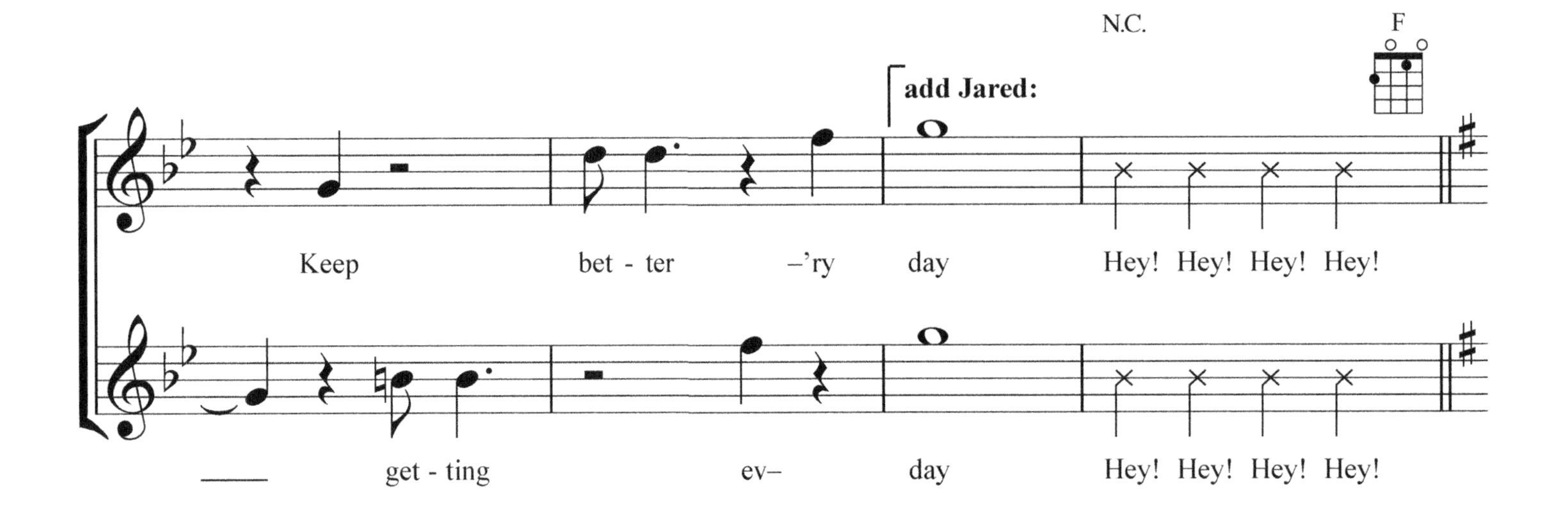
N.C.
F
add Jared:
Keep bet - ter –'ry day Hey! Hey! Hey! Hey!
get - ting ev– day Hey! Hey! Hey! Hey!

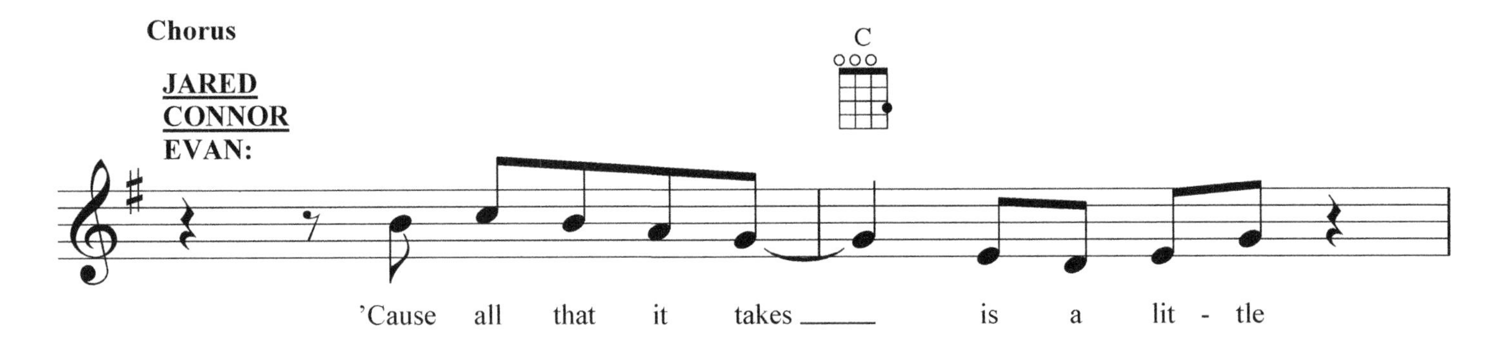
Chorus
JARED
CONNOR
EVAN:
C
'Cause all that it takes is a lit - tle

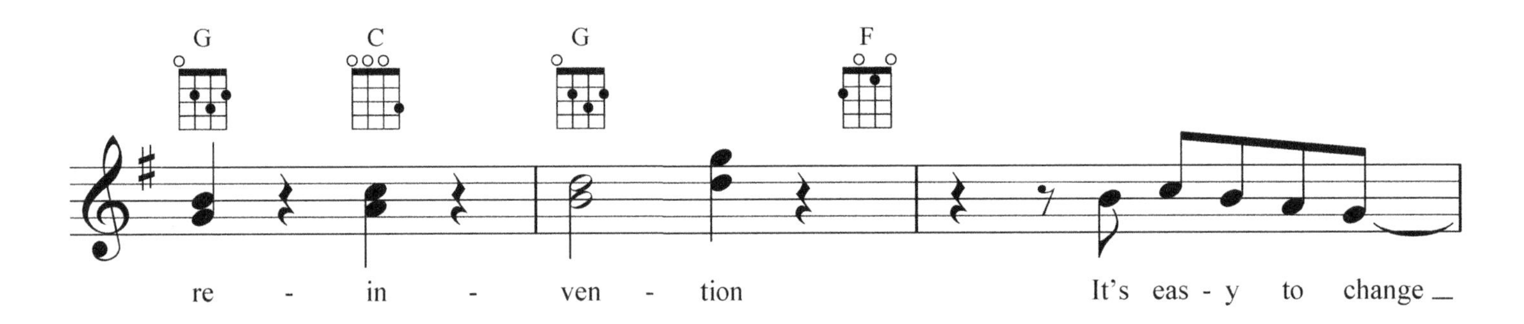
G C G F
re - in - ven - tion It's eas - y to change

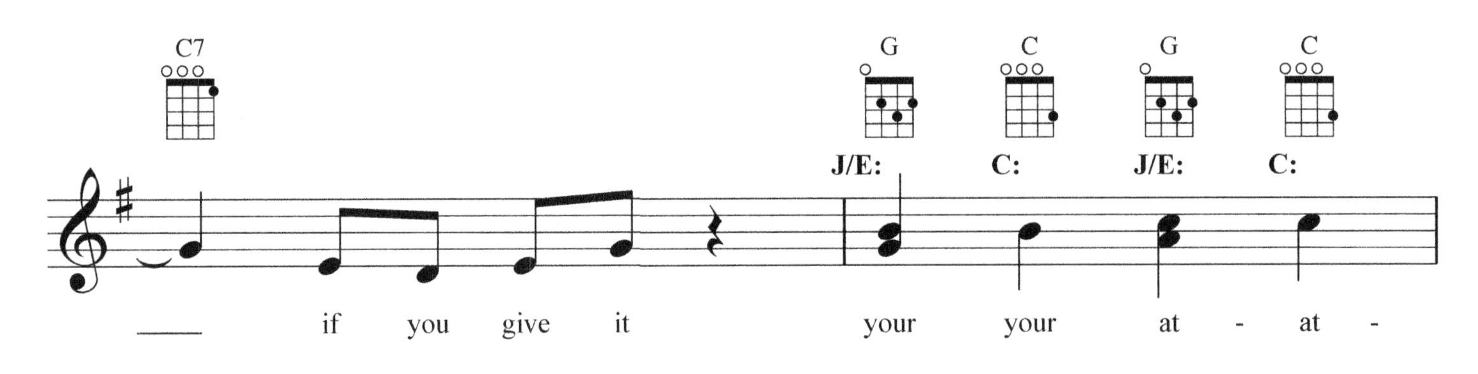
C7 G C G C
J/E: C: J/E: C:
if you give it your your at - at -

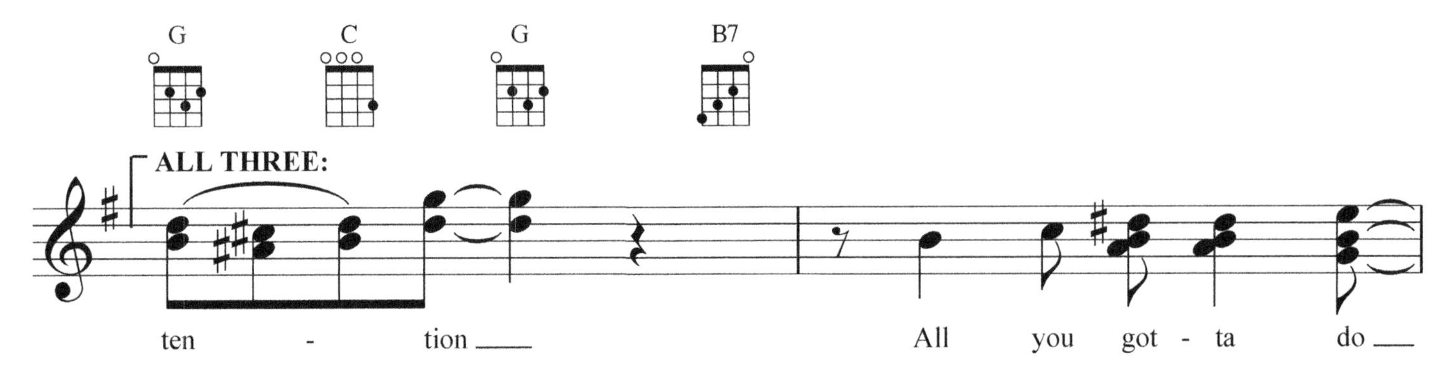
G C G B7
ALL THREE:
ten - tion All you got - ta do

Em D D7
Is just be - lieve you can be who
G G7 C G D
you wan - na be Sin - cere - ly,
C G D C
CONNOR/EVAN:
ALL THREE:
Miss you dear - ly, Sin -
Outro
G D G G7 G6 G+
EVAN:
cere - ly, Me Sin - cere - ly, Me
G G7 G6 G+ G G7
ALL THREE:
Sin - cere - ly, Me
C E♭+ G N.C. G
Sin - cere - ly, Me

Requiem

Music and Lyrics by Benj Pasek and Justin Paul

Dm7
C
F
B♭
There in my bed still sob - bing to - mor - row
Dm7
C
F
B♭
I could give in to all of the gloom But
C
B♭
C
tell me tell me what for
Pre-Chorus
A little faster
Gm7
Dm7
B♭
C
Why should I have a heav - y heart? Why should I start to break in piec - es?
Gm7
Dm7
C
Why should I go and fall a - part for you?
Chorus
Faster
F
Why should I play the griev - ing girl and

C
lie
Say - ing that I miss you and that

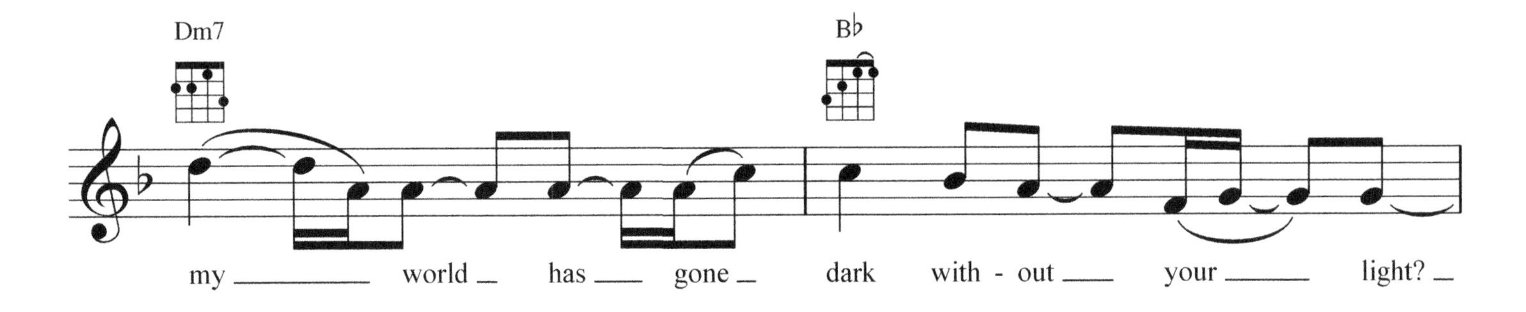
Dm7
B♭
my world has gone dark with - out your light?

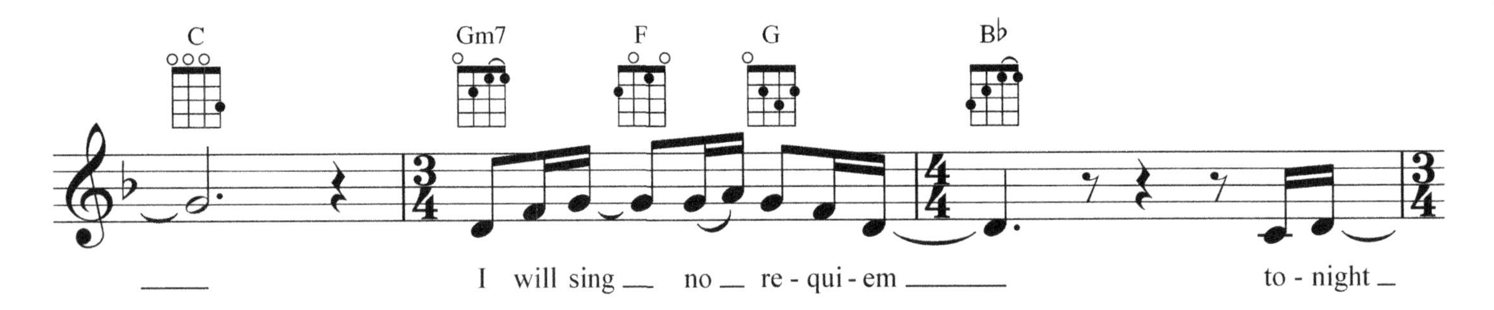
C
Gm7
F
G
B♭
I will sing no re - qui - em to - night

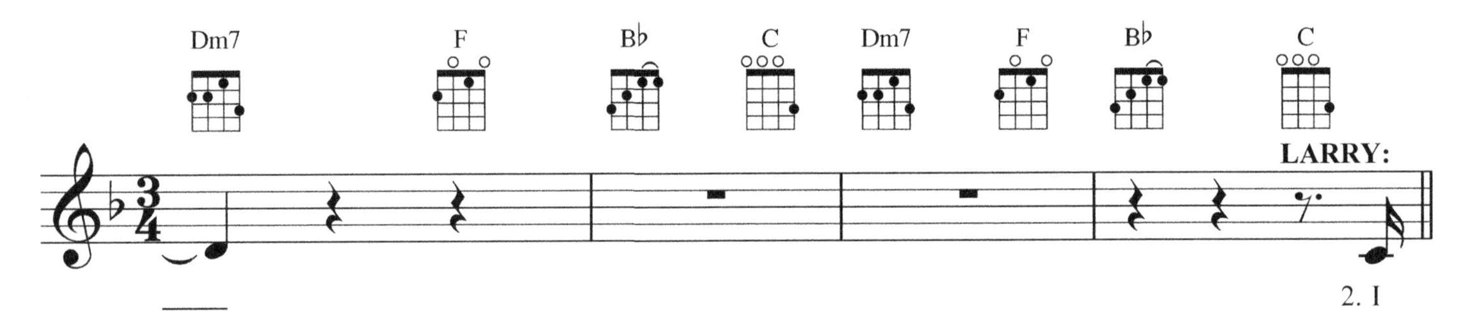
Dm7
F
B♭
C
Dm7
F
B♭
C
LARRY:
2. I

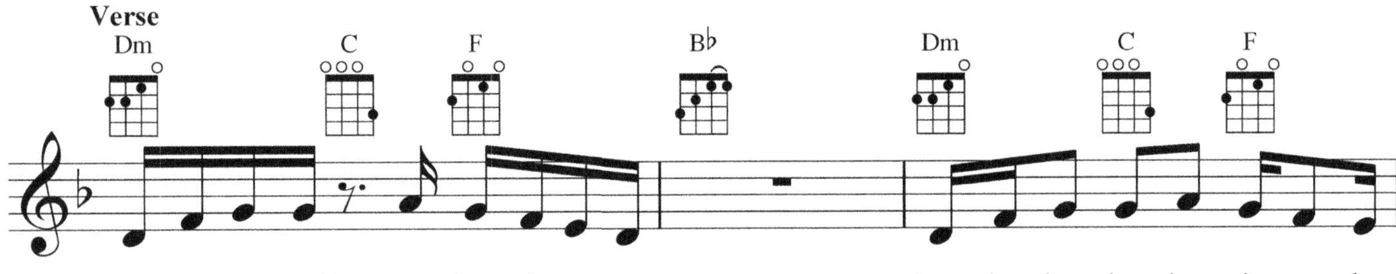
Verse
Dm
C
F
B♭
Dm
C
F
gave you the world, you threw it a - way
Leav - ing these bro - ken piec - es be -

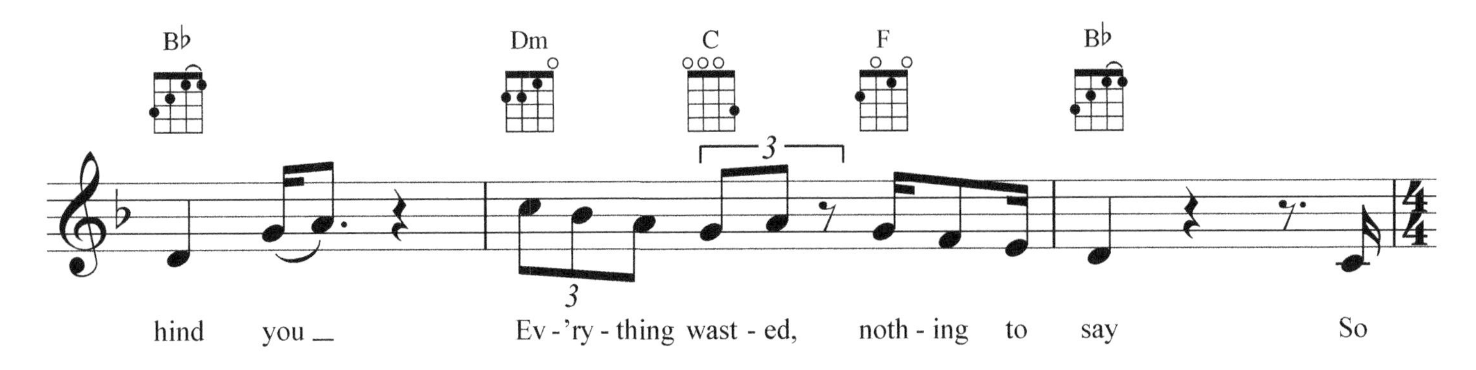
B♭
Dm
C
F
B♭
hind you
Ev - 'ry - thing wast - ed, noth - ing to say
So

Gm7
Fmaj7
5fr
CYNTHIA:
Dm7
C
Fmaj7
5fr
I can sing no re - qui - em I hear your voice and feel you

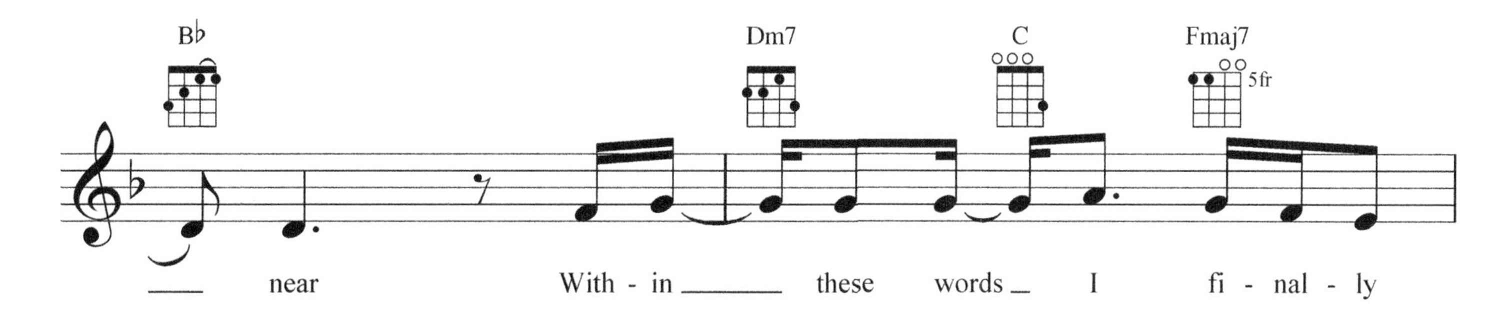
B♭
Dm7
C
Fmaj7
5fr
near With - in these words I fi - nal - ly

B♭
Dm
C
Fmaj7
5fr
find you And now that I know that you are still

G
B♭
C
here I will sing no re - qui - em to - night

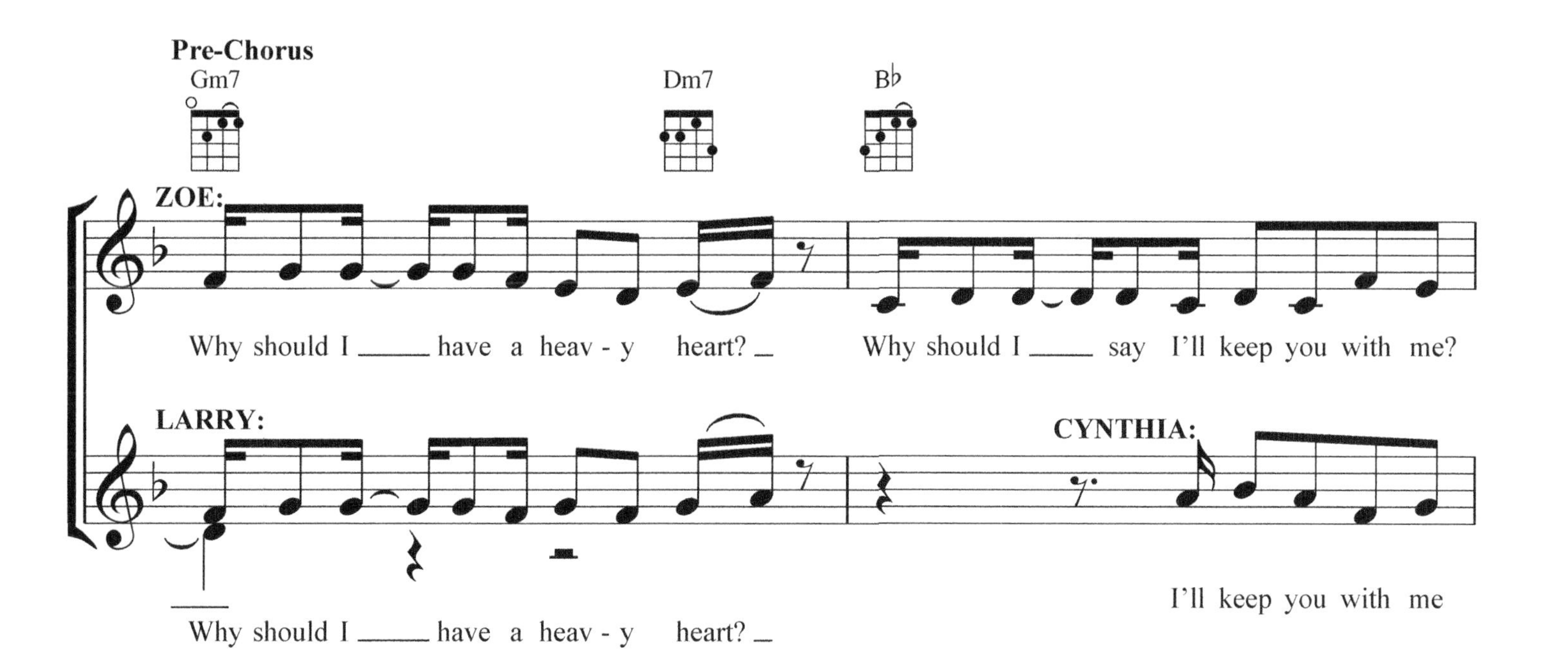
Pre-Chorus
Gm7
Dm7
B♭
ZOE:
Why should I have a heav - y heart? Why should I say I'll keep you with me?
LARRY:
CYNTHIA:
I'll keep you with me
Why should I have a heav - y heart?

Gm7
Dm7
C
ZOE:
accel.
Why should I go and fall a - part for you?
A little faster
Fmaj7
5fr
ZOE:
Why should I play the griev - ing girl and
CYNTHIA:
Ah
LARRY:
Ah
C
lie Say - ing that I miss you and that
Ah
Ah

Dm7
B♭
C
my world has gone dark with-out your light?
I can see your light
My world has gone dark
Bridge
Gm7
F
G
B♭
C
Fmaj7
5fr
ZOE:
I will sing no re-qui-em to-night 'Cause when the vil-lians
fall, the king-doms nev-er weep No one lights a can-
-dle to re-mem-ber No, no one mourns at all

Bb
C
when they lay them down to sleep So don't
Eb
Bb
F
tell me that I did-n't have it right Don't
Eb
Bb
F
tell me that it was-n't black and white Af-ter all
Eb
Bb
Eb
Bb
you put me through Don't say it was-n't true That
Freely
Gm7
Bb
you were not the mon - ster that I knew 'Cause
Outro
Tempo I
Fmaj7
5fr
C
I can-not play the griev - ing girl and lie

Dm
B♭
Say-ing that I miss you and that my world has gone dark...

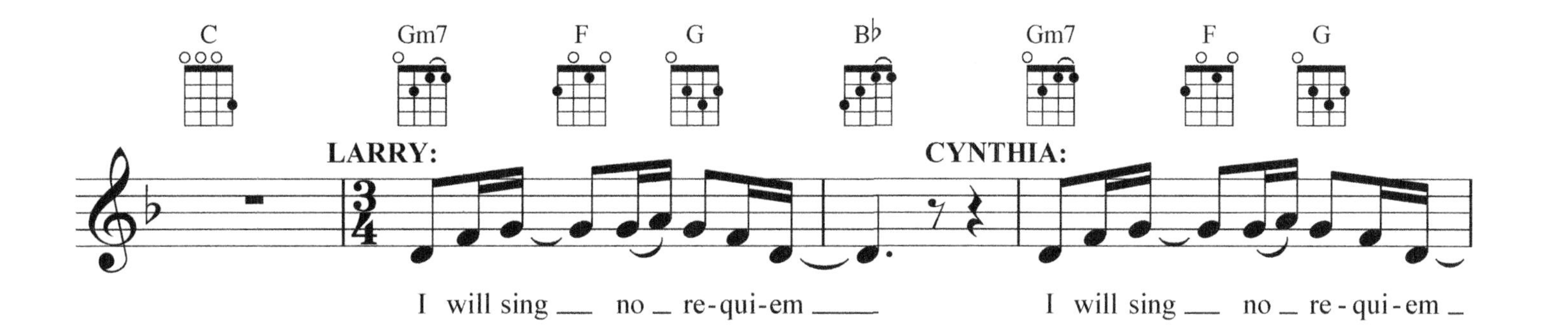
C
Gm7
F
G
B♭
Gm7
F
G
LARRY:
CYNTHIA:
I will sing no re-qui-em
I will sing no re-qui-em

B♭
Gm7
F
G
B♭
ZOE:
I will sing no re-qui-em to-

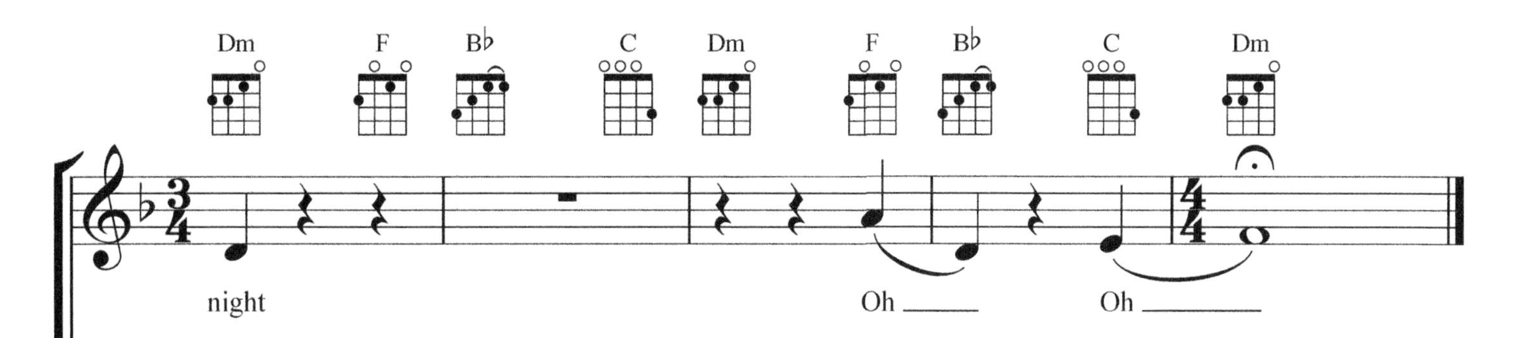
Dm
F
B♭
C
Dm
F
B♭
C
Dm
night
Oh
Oh

CYNTHIA:
Oh
Oh
Oh

LARRY:
Oh
Oh
Oh

If I Could Tell Her

Music and Lyrics by Benj Pasek and Justin Paul

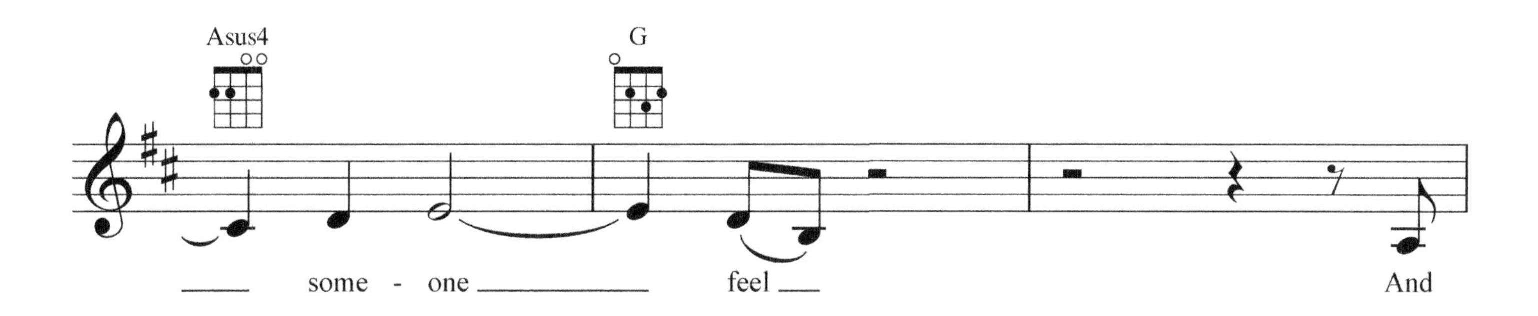
Asus4
G
some - one
feel
And

D
Asus4
Gsus2
he
knew
when - ev - er
you
get
bored

D
Asus4
you
scrib - ble
stars
on
the
cuffs
of
your
jeans

Gsus2
D
Asus4
And
he
no - ticed
that
you

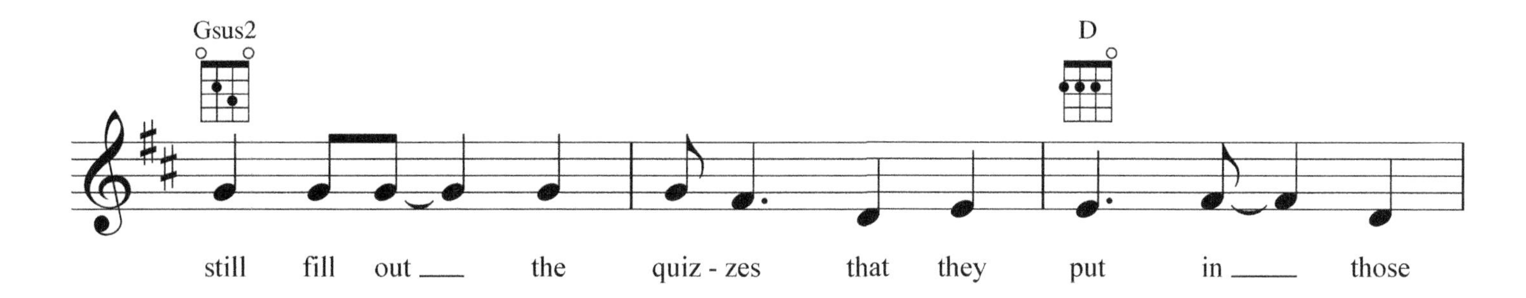
Gsus2
D
still
fill
out
the
quiz - zes
that
they
put
in
those

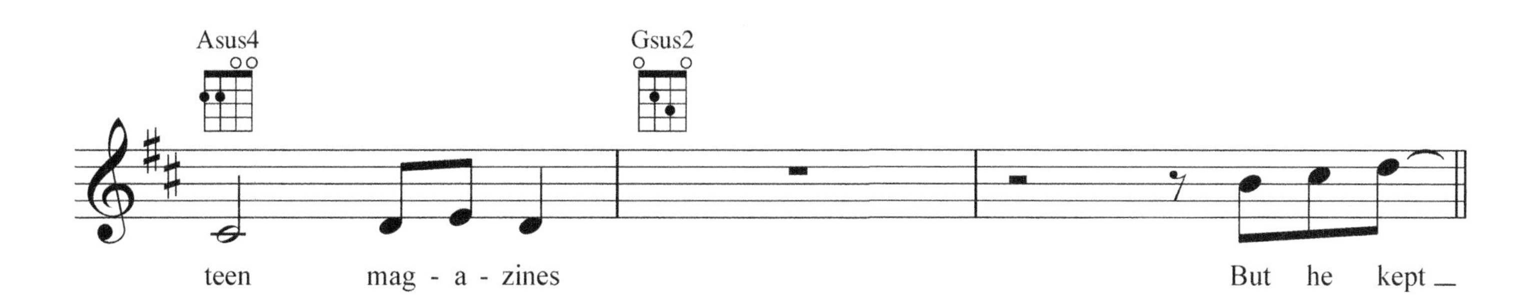
Asus4
Gsus2
teen
mag - a - zines
But
he
kept

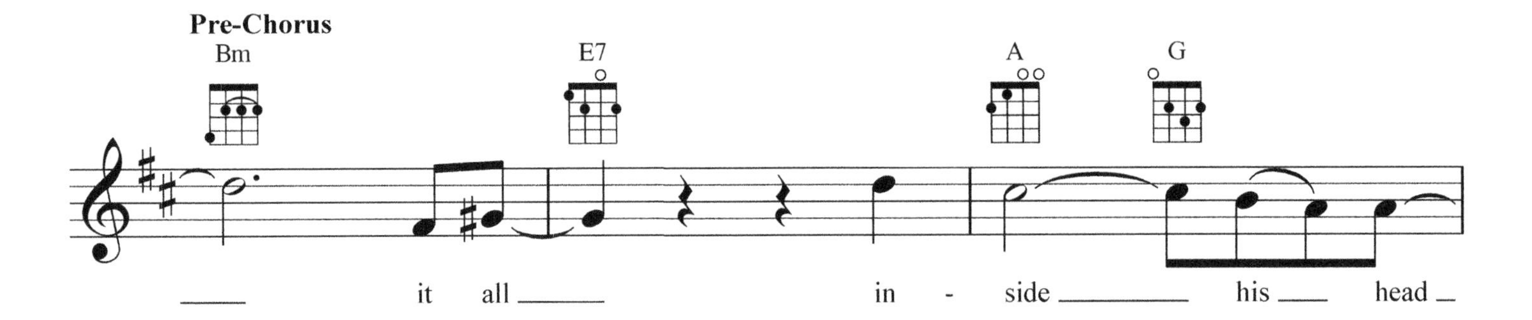
Pre-Chorus
Bm
E7
A
G
it all
in - side
his
head

D
Bm
E7
What he saw
he left
un -

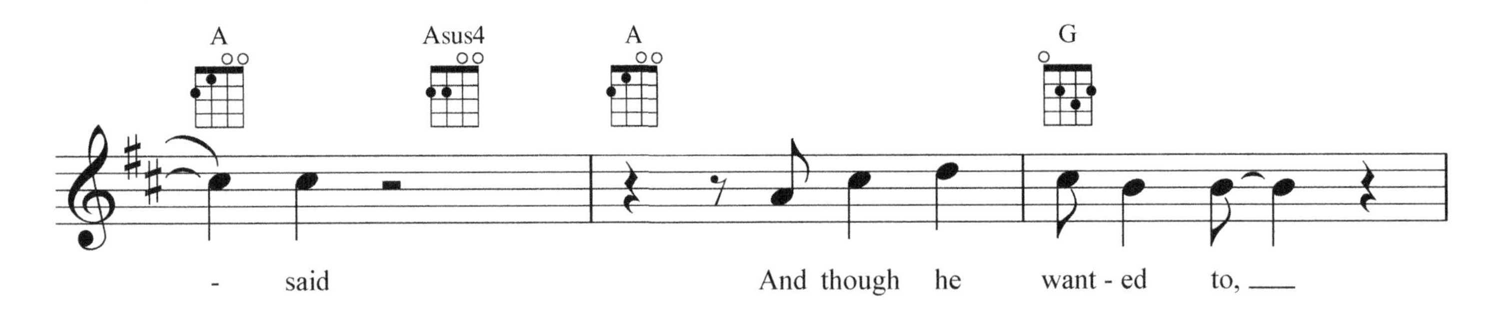
A
Asus4
A
G
- said
And though he want - ed to,

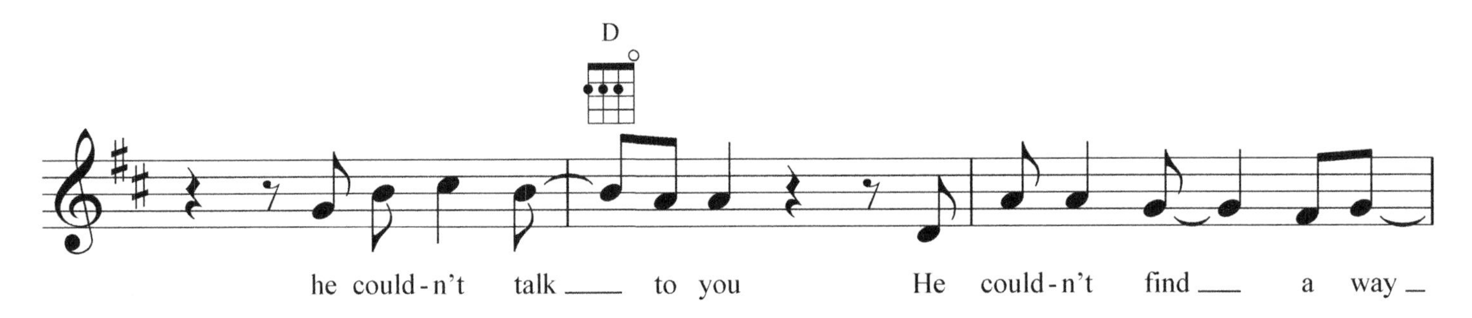
D
he could - n't talk to you
He could - n't find a way

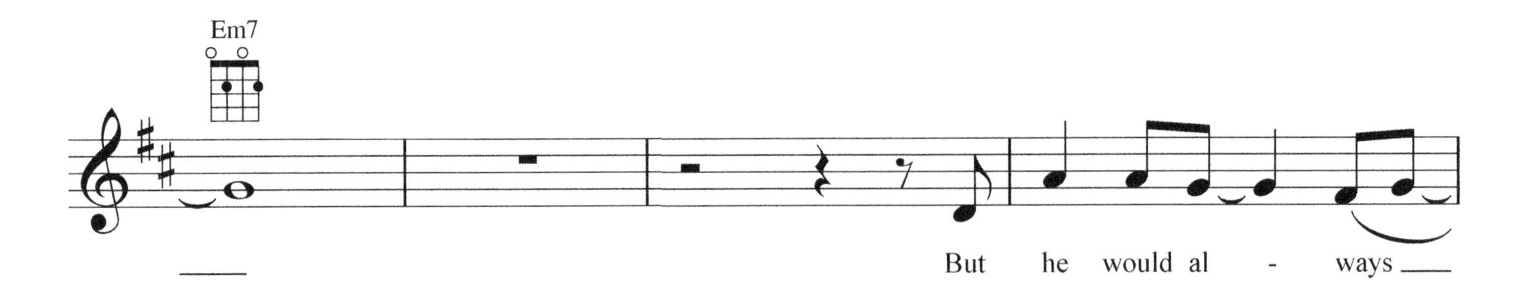
Em7
But he would al - ways

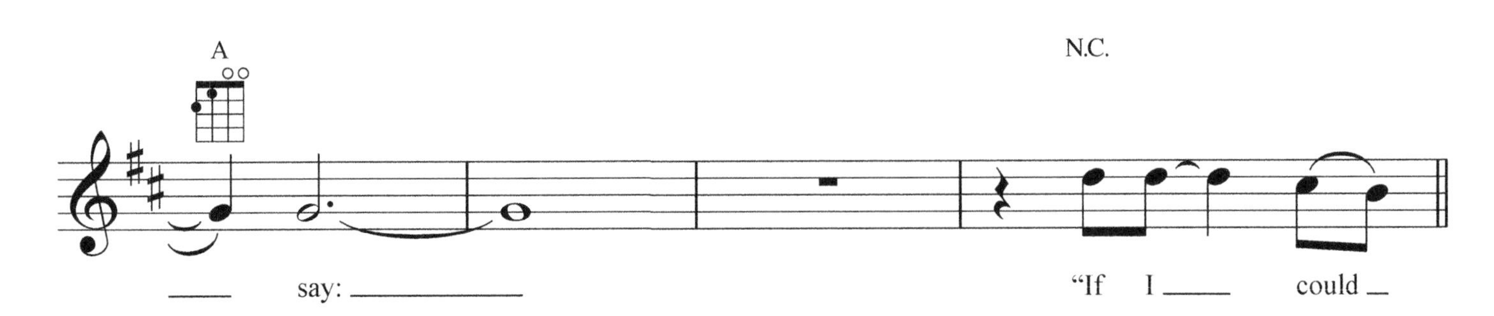
A
N.C.
say:
"If I could

Chorus
G
D
Bm
tell her Tell her ev - 'ry - thing I see

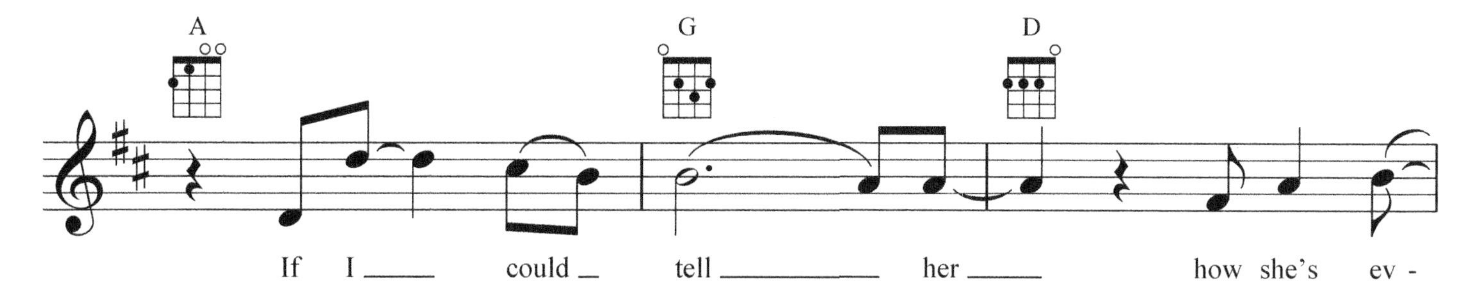
A
G
D
If I could tell her how she's ev -

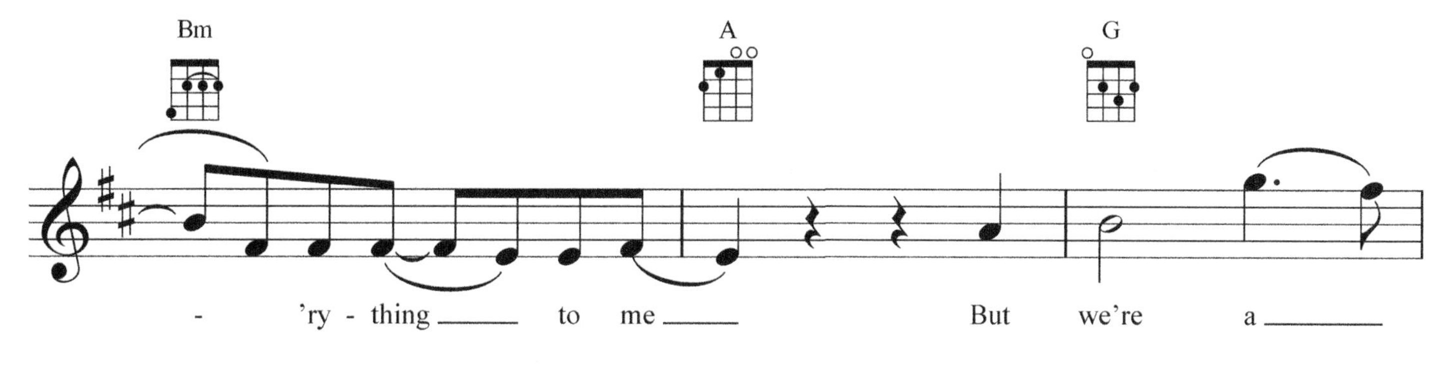
Bm
A
G
- 'ry - thing to me But we're a

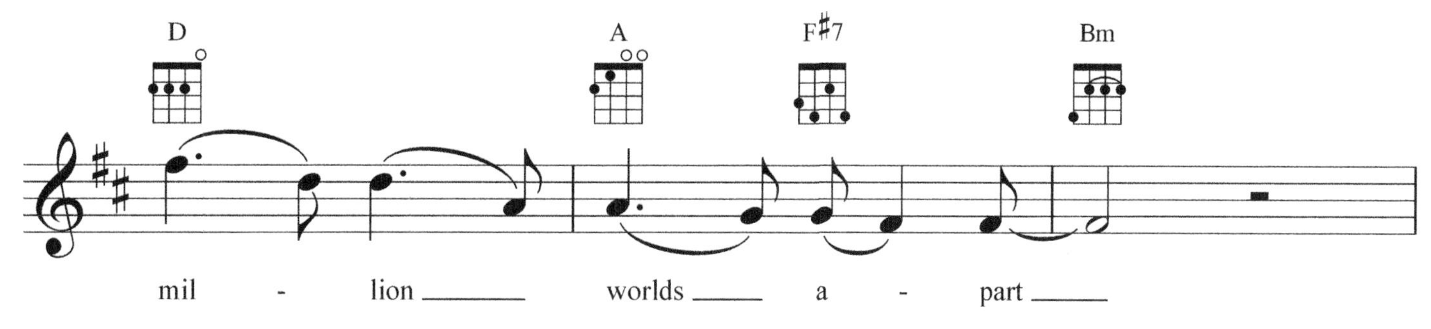
D
A
F#7
Bm
mil - lion worlds a - part

Em7
and I don't know how I would e - ven start

A7sus4
D
If I could tell her

To Coda
Em7
Gsus2
If I could
D
Em7
Gsus2
tell her"
Verse
D
Asus4
Gsus2
EVAN:
2. He thought you looked real - ly
pret - ty Err... It looked pret - ty cool when you put
D
Asus4
Gsus2
ZOE: He did?
in - di - go streaks in your hair And
D
Asus4
Gsus2
he won - dered how you learned to dance

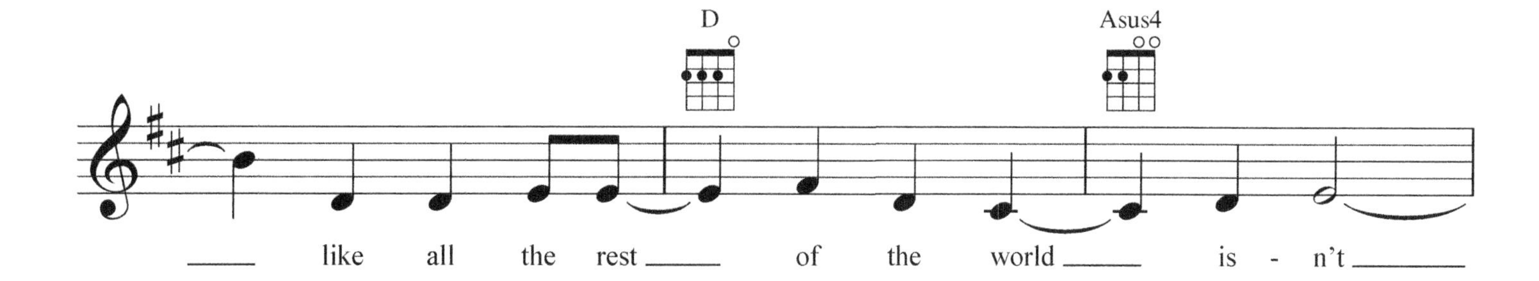
D
Asus4
like all the rest of the world is - n't

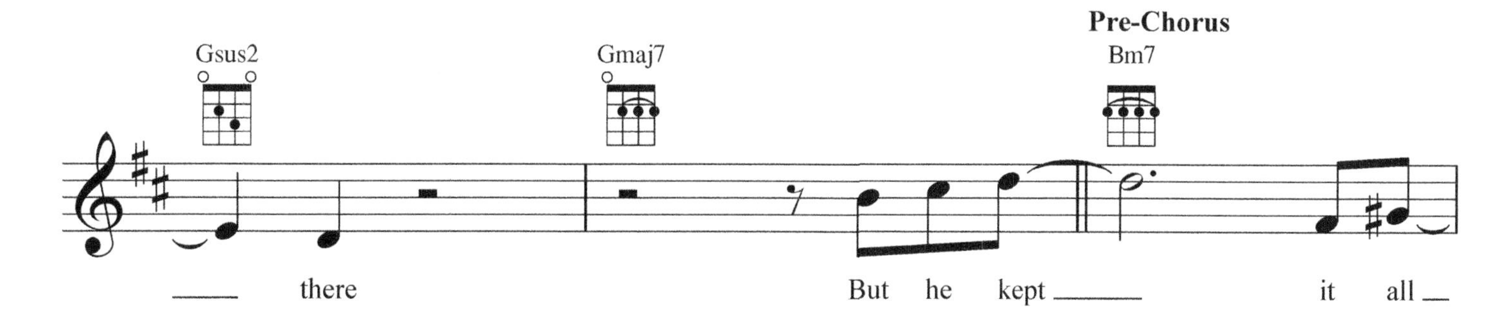
Pre-Chorus
Gsus2
Gmaj7
Bm7
there But he kept it all

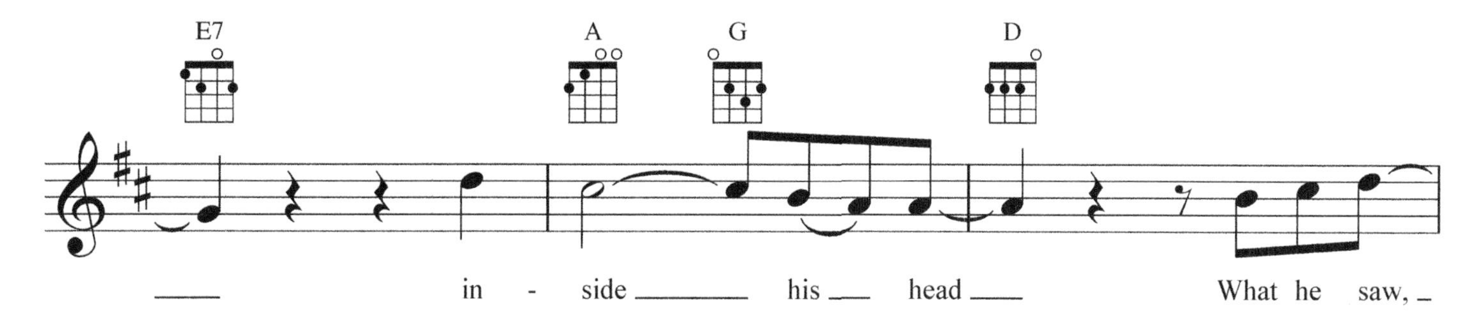
E7
A
G
D
in - side his head What he saw,

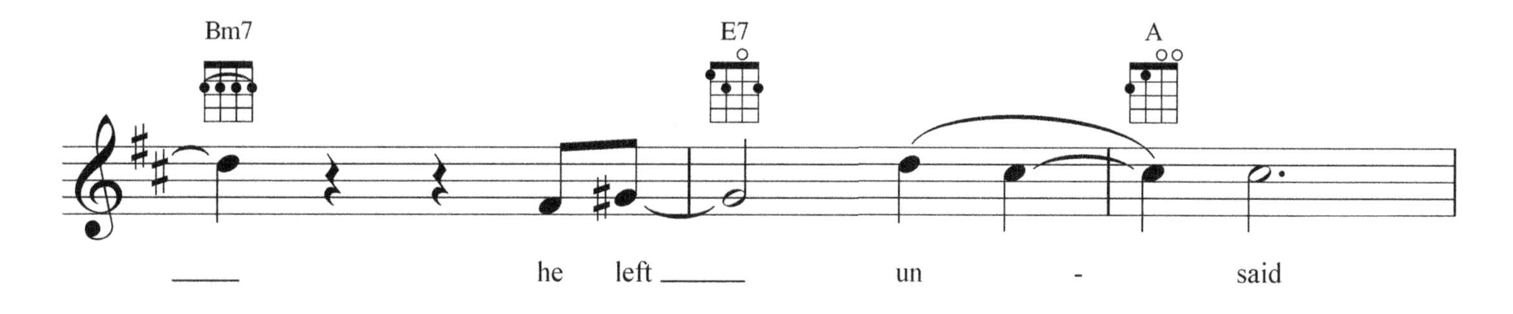
Bm7
E7
A
he left un - said

N.C.
D.S. al Coda
"If I could

Coda
If I could

Bridge
B♭
F
tell her" But whad - da - ya do when there's

C
Bb
ZOE:
this great di - vide? He just
C
Bb
EVAN:
seemed so far a - way... And whad - da - ya do
F
Dm7
C
when the dis - tance is too wide?
ZOE: It's like
Csus4
C
Csus4
C
Csus4
C
And how do you say "I
I don't know an - y - thing
Bb
love you? I
love you I

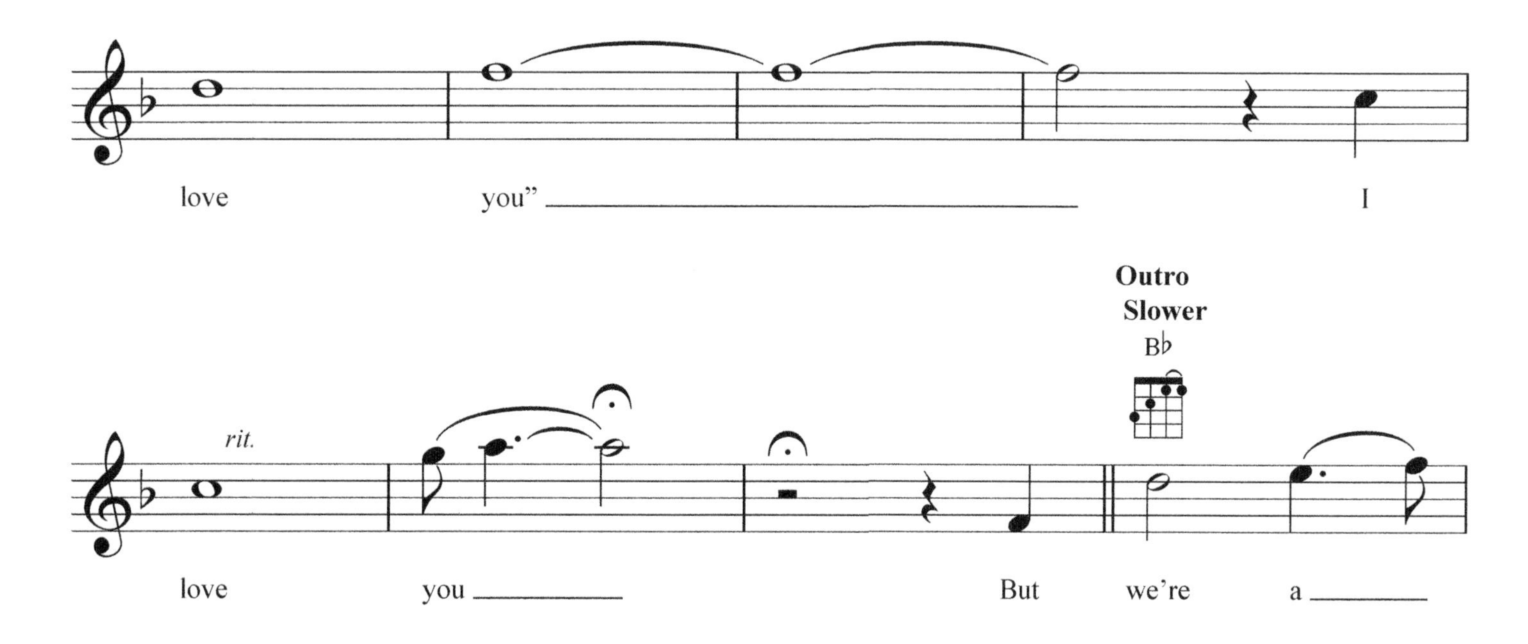
love
you"
I
Outro
Slower
B♭
rit.
love
you
But
we're
a

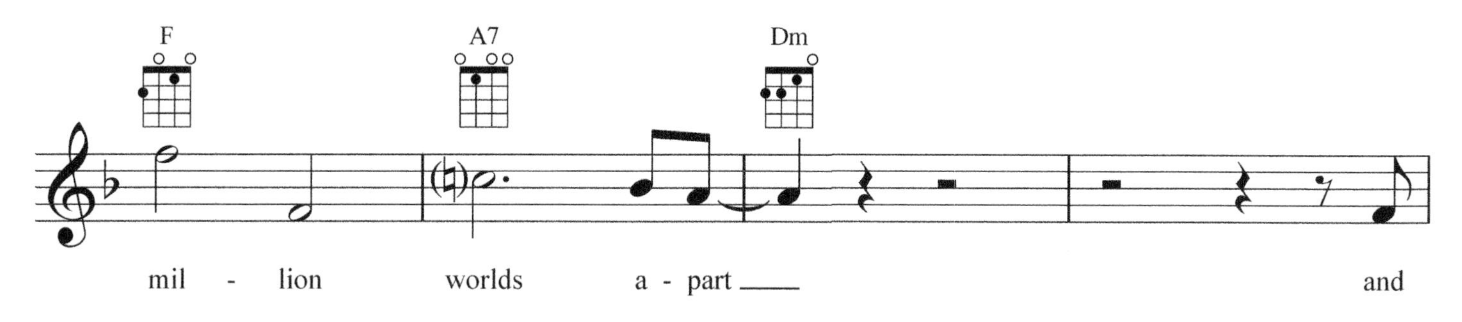
F
A7
Dm
mil - lion
worlds
a - part
and

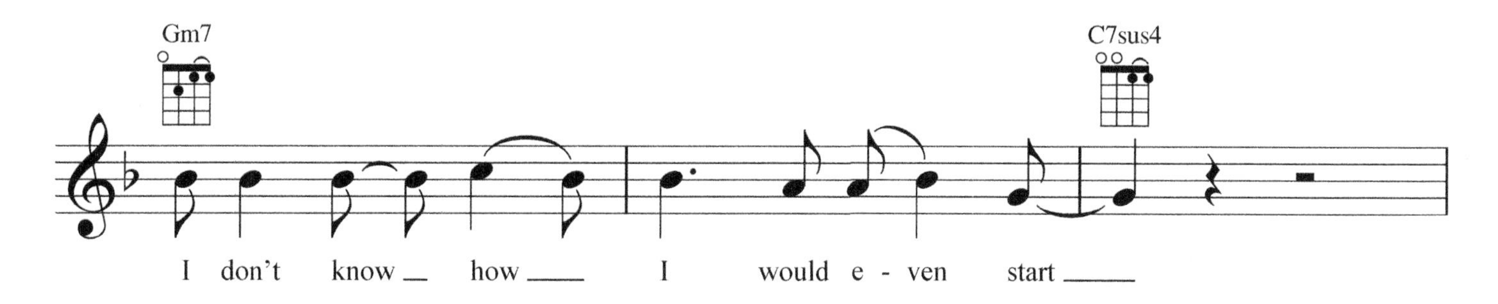
Gm7
C7sus4
I don't know how I would e - ven start

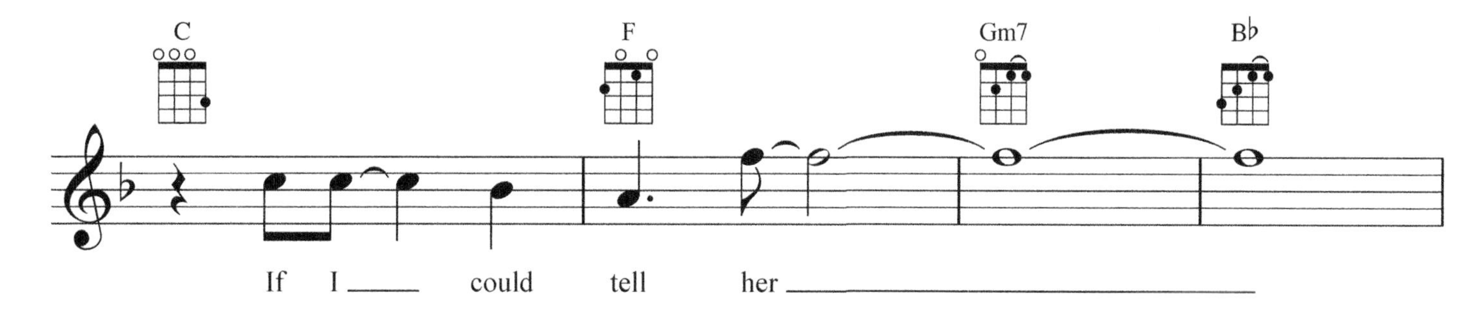
C
F
Gm7
B♭
If I could tell her

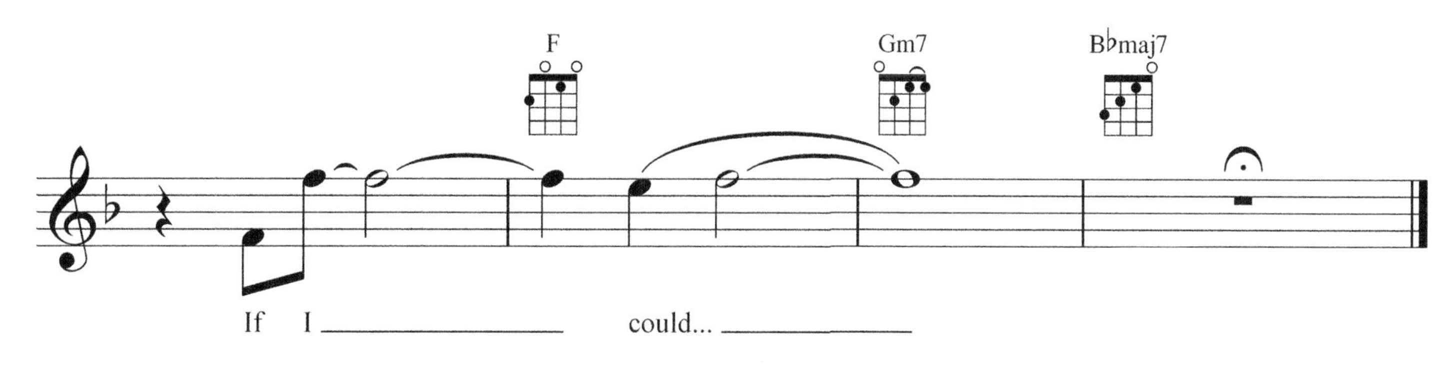
F
Gm7
B♭maj7
If I
could...

Disappear

Music and Lyrics by Benj Pasek and Justin Paul

First note

Verse
Freely

Dm7 F

CONNOR:

1. Guys like you and me, we're just the "los - ers" who keep wait - ing to be seen

C Dm7

Right? I mean... No one seems to care or stops to no -

F C

- tice that we're there so we get lost in the in - be - tween

E♭

But, if you can some - how keep them

B♭ F

think - ing of me And make me more than an a -

C
E♭
B♭
ban - doned mem - o - ry
Well, that means we mat - ter too
D♭maj7
It means some - one will see that *you* are there
Chorus
More in time
Am
F
Gsus4
G
No one de - serves to be for - got - ten
Am7
Fmaj7
5fr
Gsus4
G
No one de - serves to fade a - way
No one should
Dm7
F
C
come and go and have no one know he was ev - er e - ven
G
Am7
Fmaj7
5fr
here
No one de - serves to dis - ap - pear

Faster, with drive
G
A♭maj7
Fm
C
To dis - ap - pear
Dis - ap - pear
Verse
Fm
EVAN: It's true.
CONNOR:
2. E - ven if you've al - ways been that
A♭
3fr
E♭
add EVAN:
CONNOR:
"bare - ly in the back - ground" kind of guy
you still mat - ter And
Fm
A♭
3fr
e - ven if you're some - bod - y who can't es - cape the feel - ing that the
E♭
world's passed you by
If you
EVAN:
You still mat - ter

G♭
D♭
nev - er get a - round to do - ing some re - mark - a - ble thing

A♭
3fr
E♭
G♭
add EVAN:
EVAN:
That does - n't mean that you're not worth re - mem - ber - ing

D♭
Emaj7
4fr
CONNOR:
Think of the peo - ple who need to know
They need

So you need to show them
to know
I need to show

Chorus

Cm7
A♭
3fr
that no one de - serves to be for - got -
them that no one de - serves to be for - got -

B♭
- ten
- ten No one de - serves to be for - got -

Cm7
A♭
3fr
No one de - serves to fade a - way
- ten No one de - serves to fade a - way

B♭
No one should
to fade a - way No one should

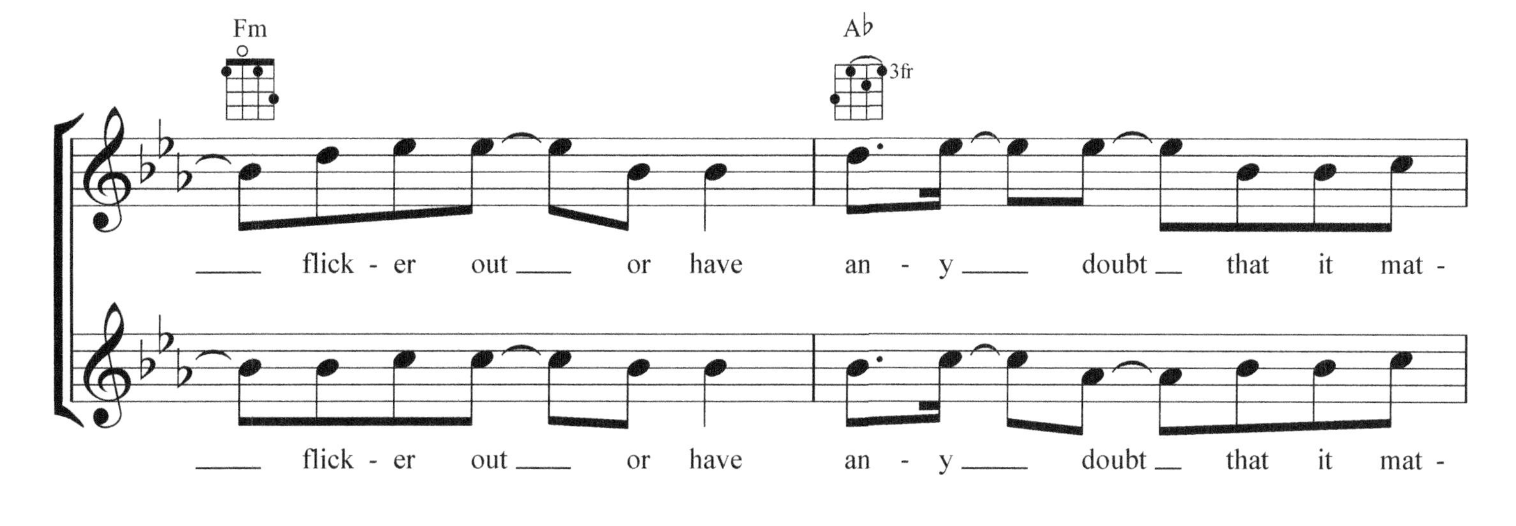
Fm
A♭
3fr
flick - er out or have an - y doubt that it mat -
flick - er out or have an - y doubt that it mat -

E♭
B♭
ters that they are here
ters that they are here
No one de - serves

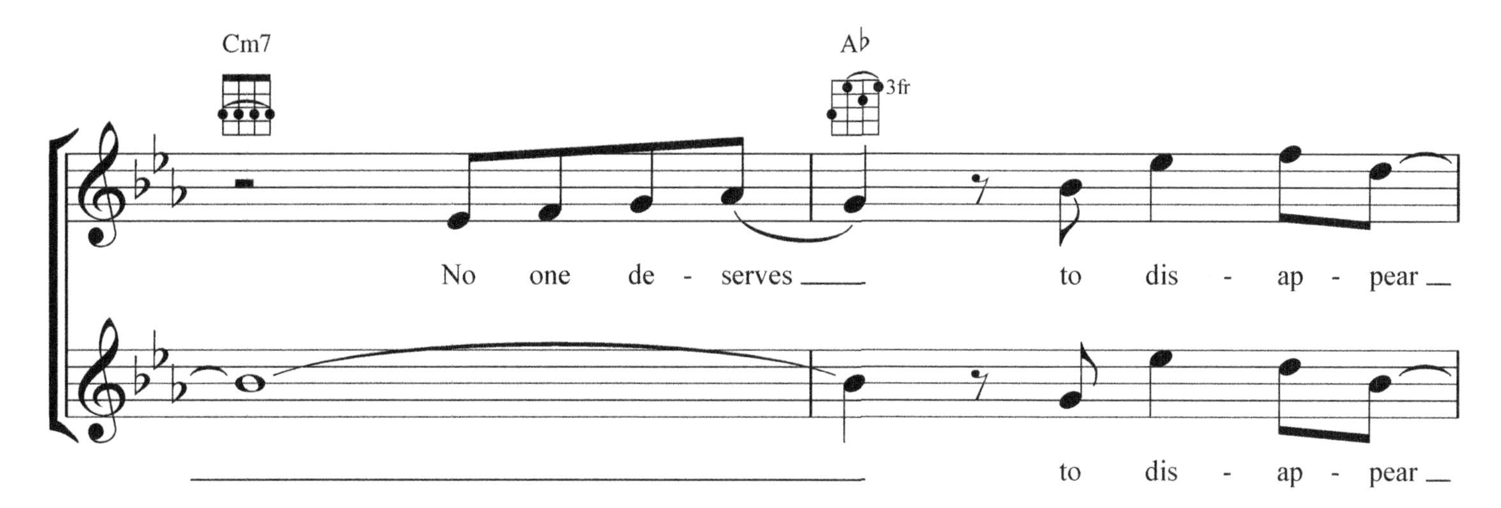
Cm7
A♭
3fr
No one de - serves to dis - ap - pear
to dis - ap - pear

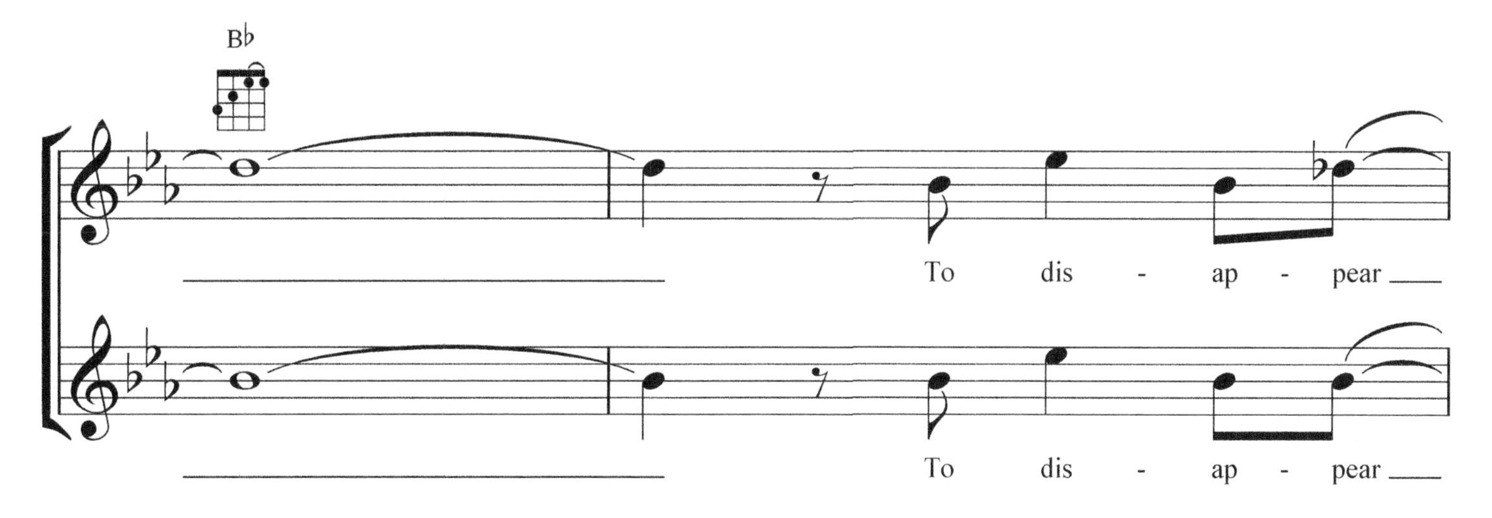
B♭
To dis - ap - pear
To dis - ap - pear

Bmaj7
A♭m7
N.C.
CONNOR:
Dis - ap - pear
When you're
Dis - ap - pear

Bridge

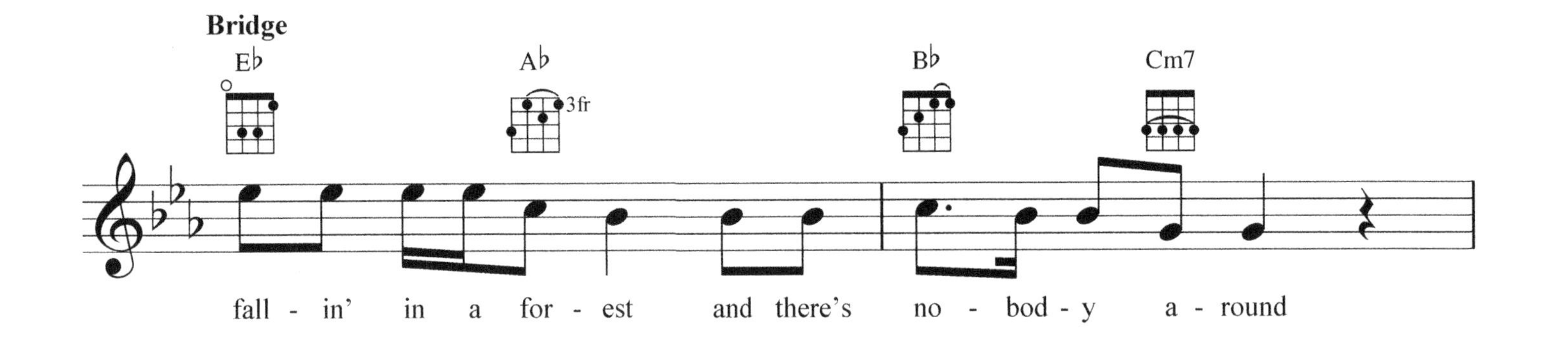
E♭
A♭
3fr
B♭
Cm7
fall - in' in a for - est and there's no - bod - y a - round

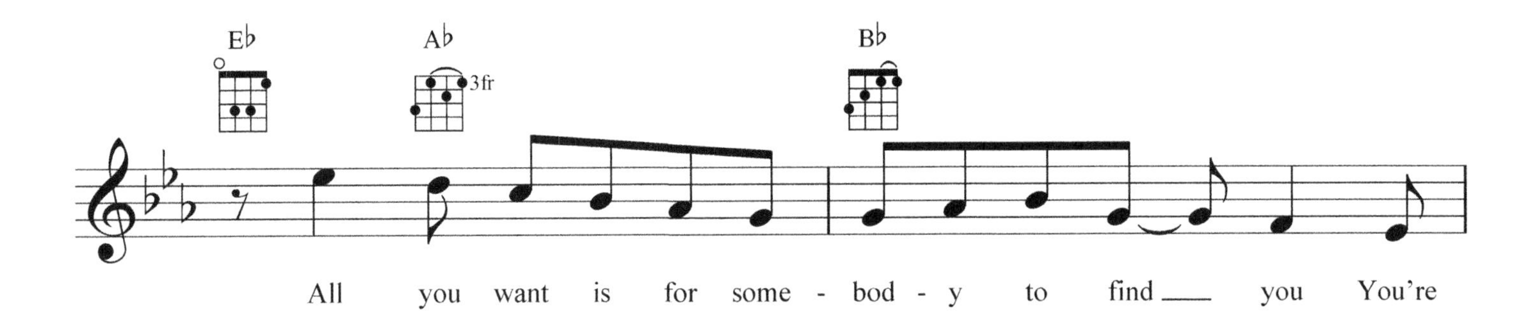
E♭
A♭
3fr
B♭
All you want is for some - bod - y to find you You're

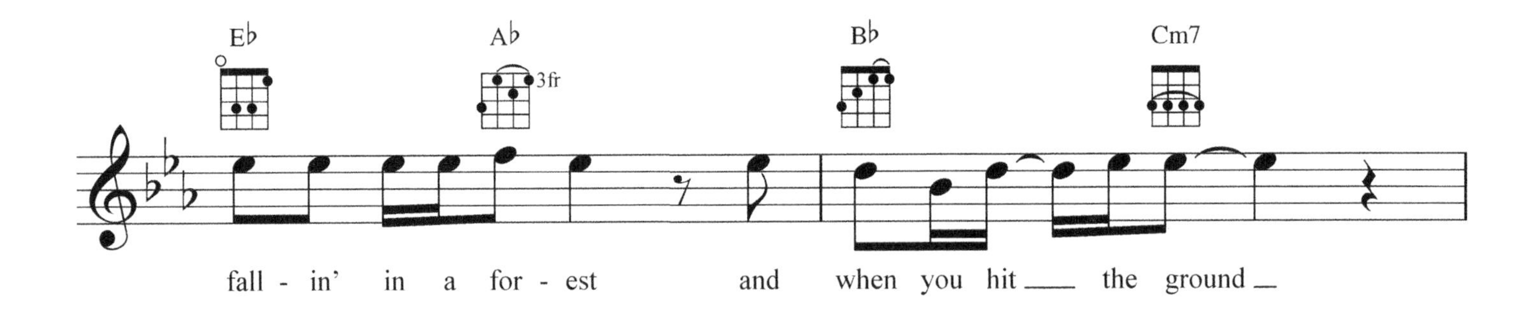
E♭
A♭
3fr
B♭
Cm7
fall - in' in a for - est and when you hit the ground

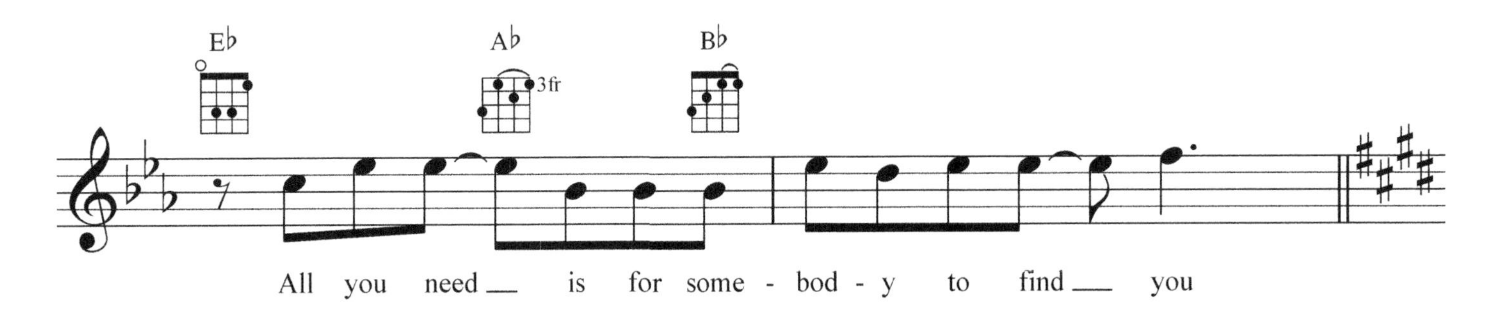
E♭
A♭
3fr
B♭
All you need is for some - bod - y to find you

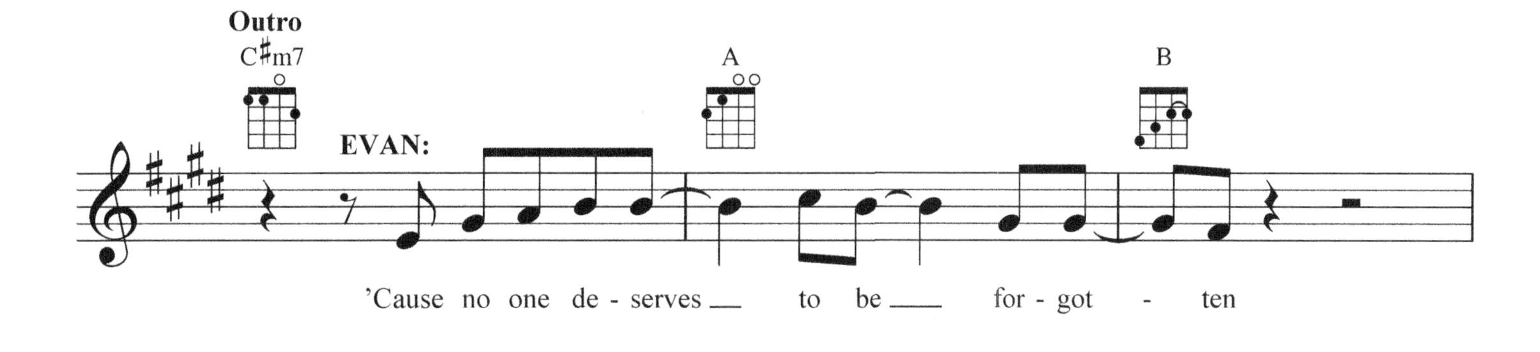
Outro
C♯m7
A
B
EVAN:
'Cause no one de - serves to be for - got - ten

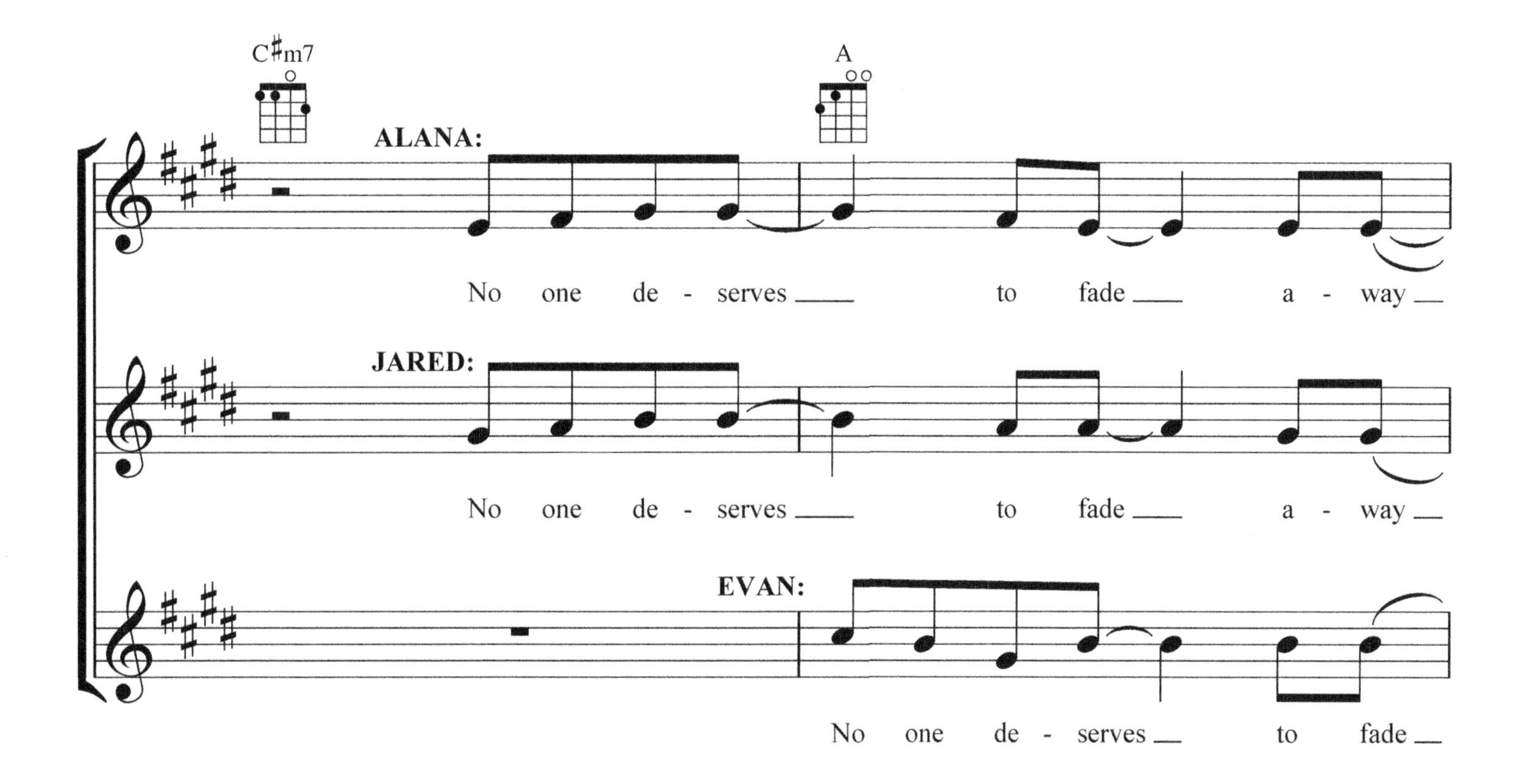
C♯m7
A
ALANA:
No one de - serves to fade a - way
JARED:
No one de - serves to fade a - way
EVAN:
No one de - serves to fade

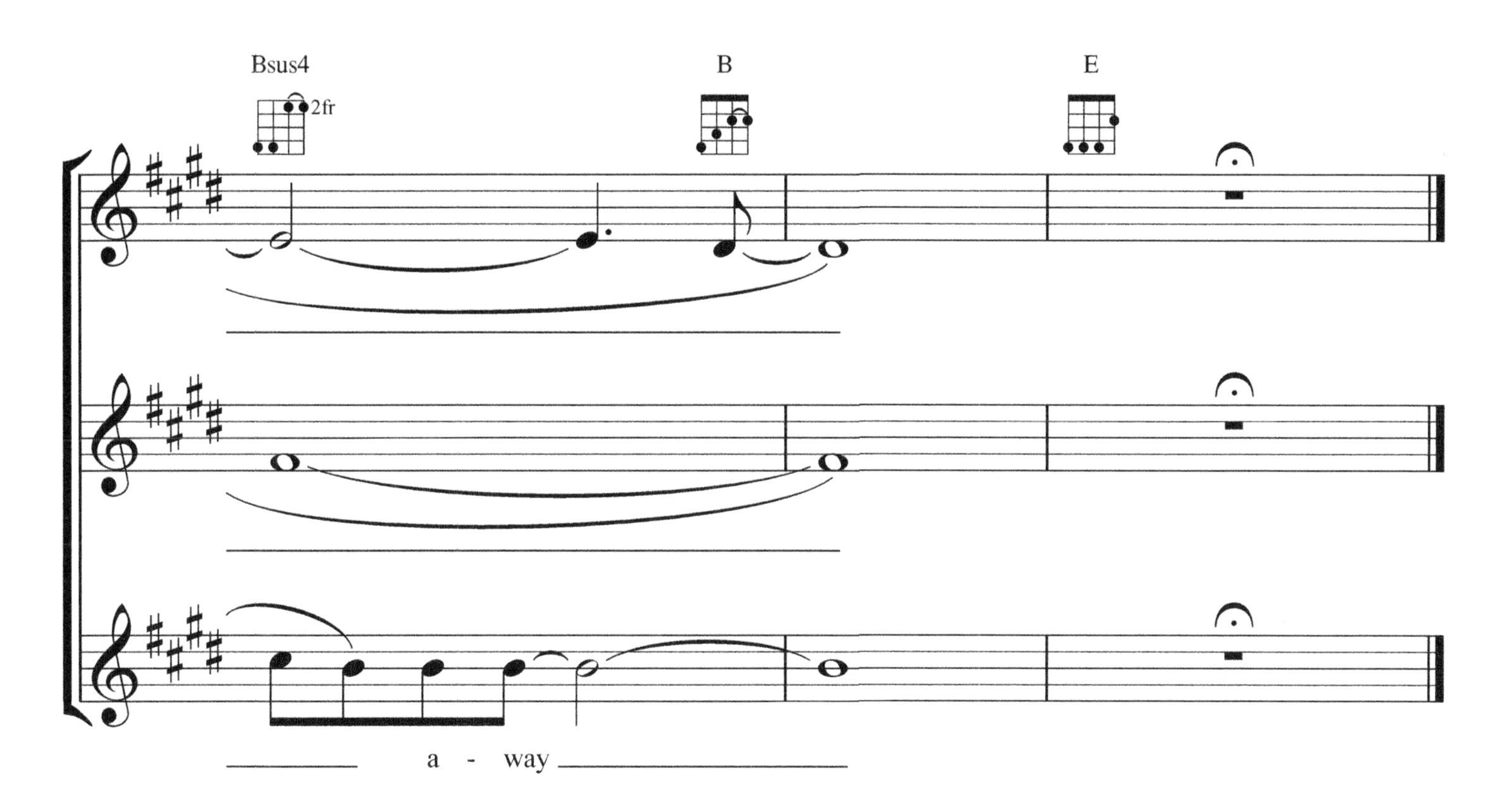
Bsus4
2fr
B
E
a - way

You Will Be Found

Music and Lyrics by Benj Pasek and Justin Paul

Am
F
C
a - way
May - be there's a rea - son to be - lieve
G
Am
F
C
you'll be o - kay
'Cause when you don't feel strong e - nough
Am
F
to stand
You can reach, reach out
C
Pre-Chorus
Gsus4
C
F
your hand,
and
Oh
F
Gsus4
C
some - one will come run - nin'
And I
know
they'll take you
Chorus
More relaxed, quasi rubato
F
C
home
E - ven when the dark comes crash - in' through

G
When you need a friend to car - ry you

Am
And when you're bro - ken on the ground,

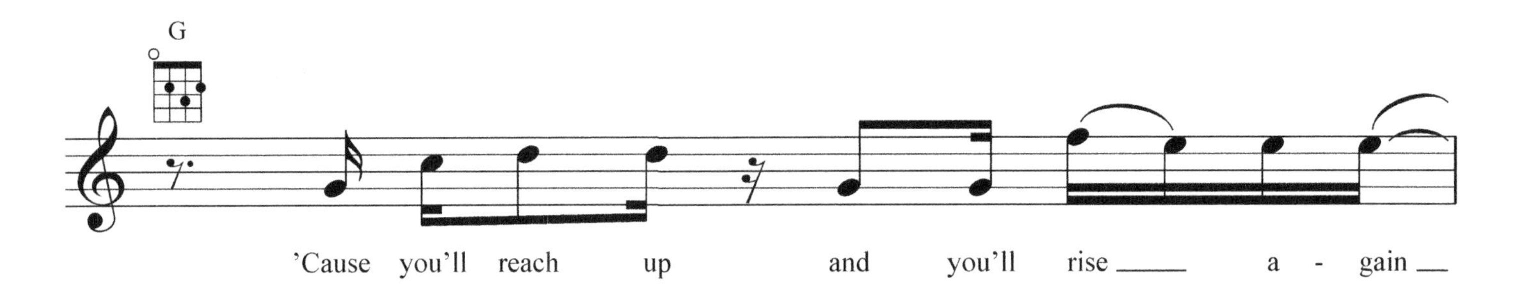
A tempo
F
C
you will be found
So let the sun come stream - in' in

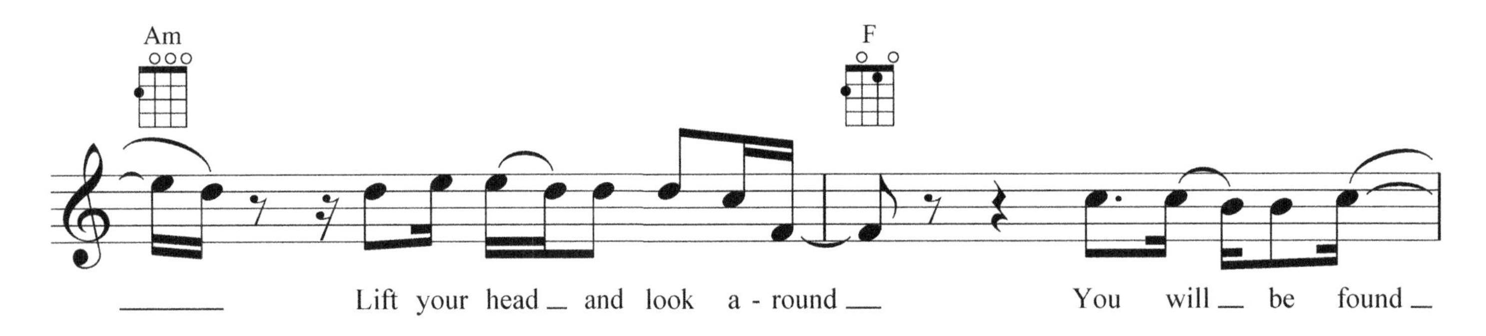
G
'Cause you'll reach up and you'll rise a - gain
Am
F
Lift your head and look a - round
You will be found

C
Gsus4
You will be found

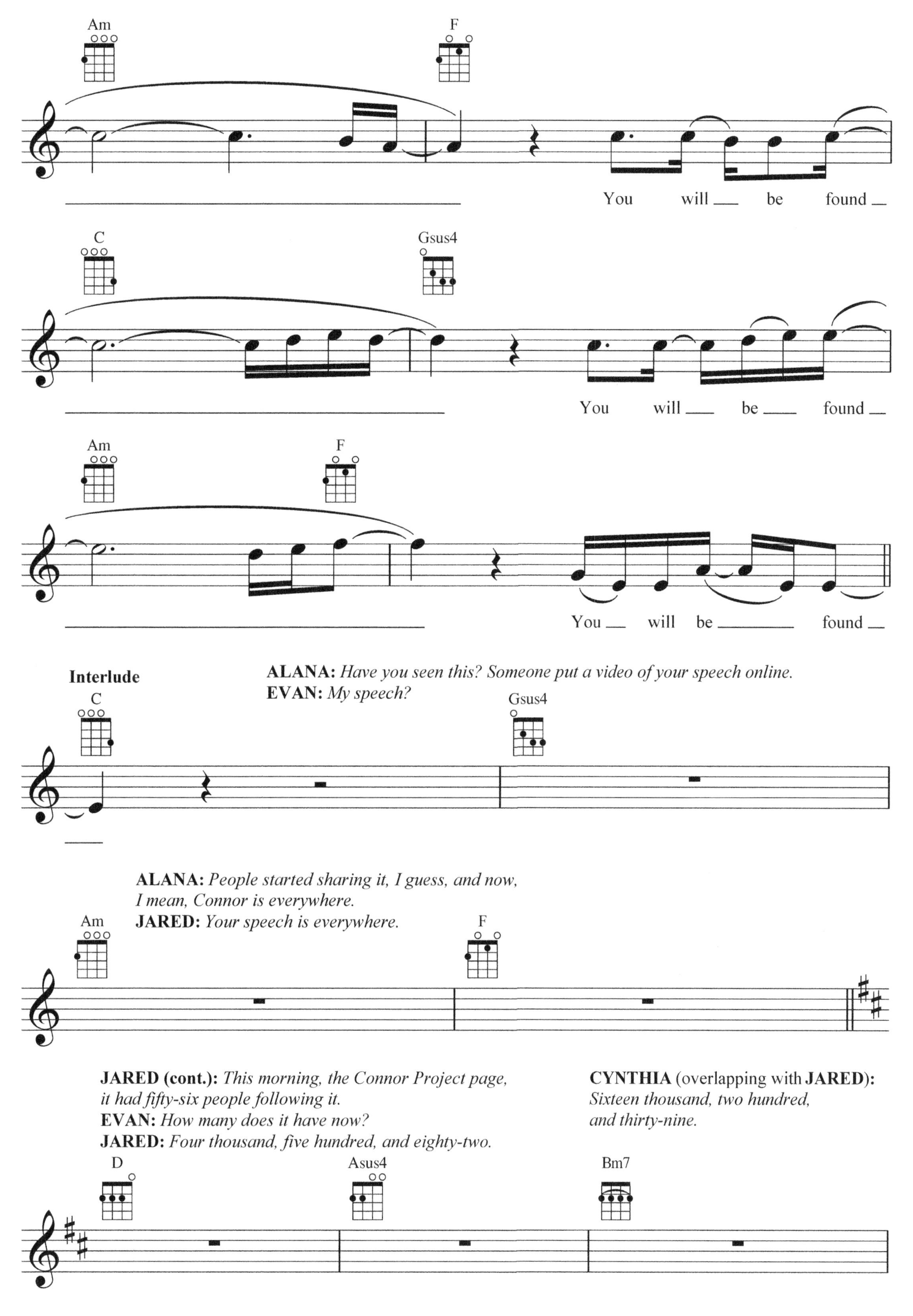
Am
F
You will be found
C
Gsus4
You will be found
Am
F
You will be found
Interlude
ALANA: Have you seen this? Someone put a video of your speech online.
EVAN: My speech?
C
Gsus4
ALANA: People started sharing it, I guess, and now, I mean, Connor is everywhere.
JARED: Your speech is everywhere.
Am
F
JARED (cont.): This morning, the Connor Project page, it had fifty-six people following it.
EVAN: How many does it have now?
JARED: Four thousand, five hundred, and eighty-two.
CYNTHIA (overlapping with JARED): Sixteen thousand, two hundred, and thirty-nine.
D
Asus4
Bm7

Gsus2
A
EVAN: I don't understand. What happened?
CYNTHIA: You did.
ALANA:
2. There's a
Verse
Bm7
Gsus2
D
A
place where we don't have to feel un - known
Bm7
Gsus2
D
A
And ev-'ry time that you call out you're a lit - tle less a - lone
Bm7
Gsus2
D
A
JARED:
If you on - ly say the word
JARED
ALANA:
From a - cross
Bm7
Gsus2
D
the si - lence your voice is heard
Chorus
D
COMPANY & VIRTUAL COMMUNITY:
E - ven when the dark comes crash - in' through

A
When you need a friend to car - ry you

Bm7
When you're bro - ken on the ground

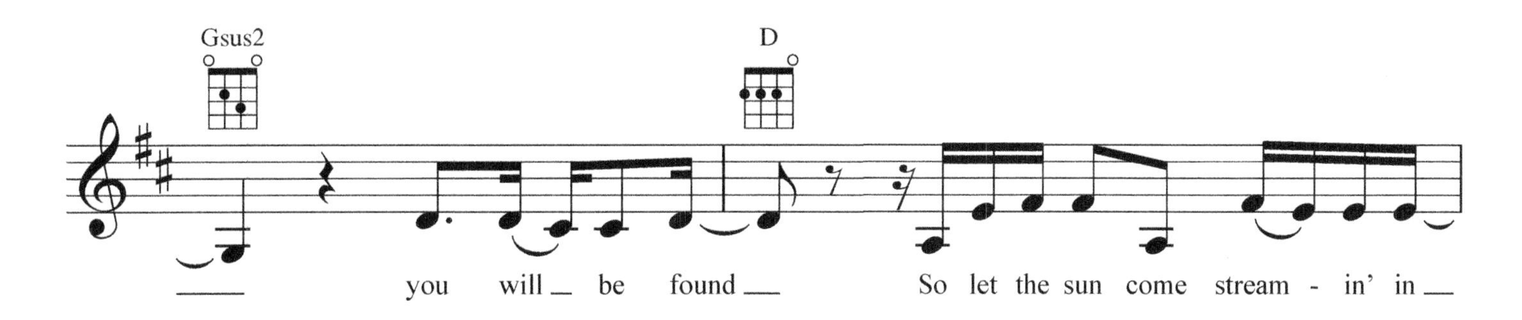
Gsus2
D
you will be found
So let the sun come stream - in' in

A
'Cause you'll reach up and you'll rise a - gain

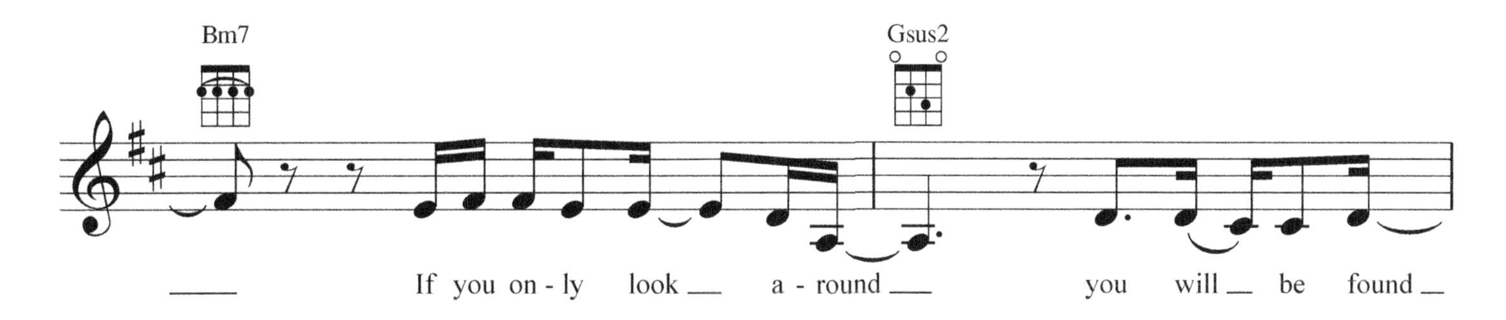
Bm7
Gsus2
If you on - ly look a - round
you will be found

D
Asus4
D
you will be found

To Coda
Bridge
Gsus2
C
Out of the shad - dows the
Gsus2
morn - ing is break - ing and all
D
A
is new All is new It's
C
fill - in' up the emp - ty and
Gsus2
D
sud - den - ly I see that all is new All
A
D.S. al Coda
is new
Coda
D

To Break in a Glove

Music and Lyrics by Benj Pasek and Justin Paul

LARRY: *Shaving cream.*
EVAN: *Shaving cream?*
LARRY: *Oh yeah. You rub that in for about five minutes. Tie it all up with rubber bands, put it under your mattress, and sleep on it. And you do that for at least a week. Every day. Consistent.*

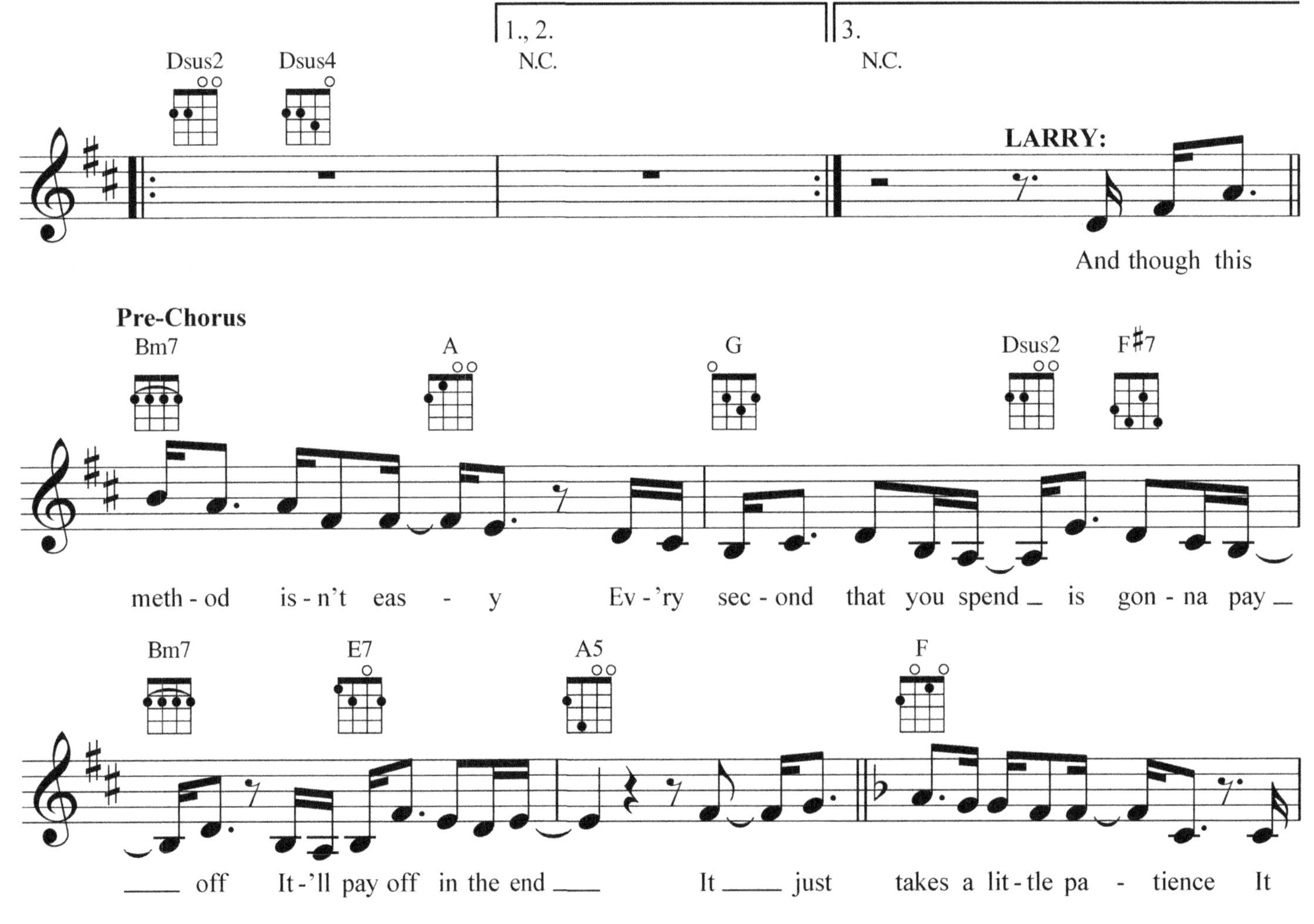

LARRY: *With something like this, you have to be ready to put in the work. Make the commitment...*

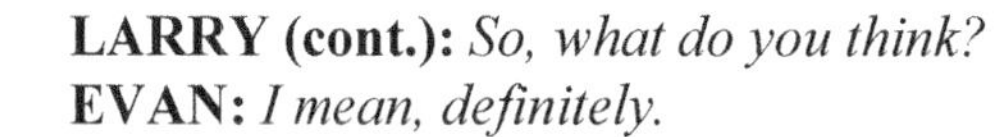

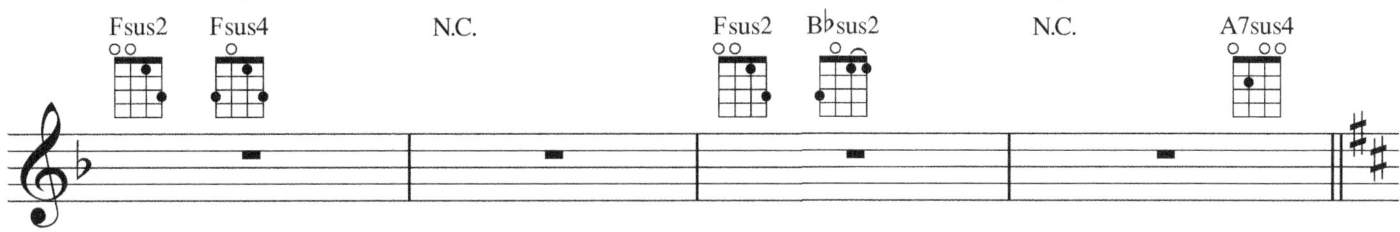

Verse
Dsus2
E7
LARRY:
3. Some peo - ple say, "Just use a mi - cro - wave Or try that
G
Dsus2
Dsus4
[he laughs]
'Run - it - through - hot - wa - ter' tech - nique" Well,
Dsus2
E
they can gloat a - bout the time they save 'Til they
Gsus2
Dsus2
D
Dsus2
got - ta buy an - oth - er glove next week It just
Chorus
F
C
takes a lit - tle pa - tience It takes a lit - tle time
EVAN:
It takes a lit - tle pa - tience It takes a lit - tle time

F7
Bbmaj7
A lit-tle per-se-ver-ance And a lit-tle up - hill climb And it's the hard
Per-se-ver-ance A lit-tle up - hill climb
F
Bm7b5
BOTH:
way But it's the right way The
Bb
C7sus4
LARRY:
right way 'Cause there's a
Ab
3fr
Eb
right way In ev - 'ry - thing you do
Fm
Db
EVAN
LARRY:
Keep that grit Fol - low through
EVAN: Keep that grit

E♭ D♭ E♭ A♭ 3fr E♭
LARRY:
E - ven when ev - 'ry - one a - round you thinks you're cra - zy
D♭ E♭
E - ven when ev - 'ry - one a - round you lets things go
D♭ E♭
Wheth - er you're prep - ping for some test Or you're
D♭ E♭ C7
miles from some goal Or you're just try - ing to do what's best For a
Fm A♭ 3fr D♭
kid who's lost con - trol You do the hard
Colla voce
A♭ 3fr Dm7♭5
thing 'Cause that's the right thing Yeah, that's the

D♭
B♭m7
right thing
EVAN: Connor was really lucky.
To have a dad that...a dad who cared so much.
About...taking care of stuff.
Tempo I
Fsus2
Fsus4
N.C.
LARRY: Shaving cream. Rubber bands.
Mattress. Repeat. Got it?
EVAN: Got it.
Fsus2
B♭add9
N.C.
LARRY:
It's the hard
Outro
Slower
F
Bm7♭5
EVAN:
LARRY
EVAN:
way But it's the right way The
Gm7
C7sus4
right way To break in a glove
Tempo I
Fsus2
Fsus4
F
LARRY: You're good to go.

Only Us

Music and Lyrics by Benj Pasek and Justin Paul

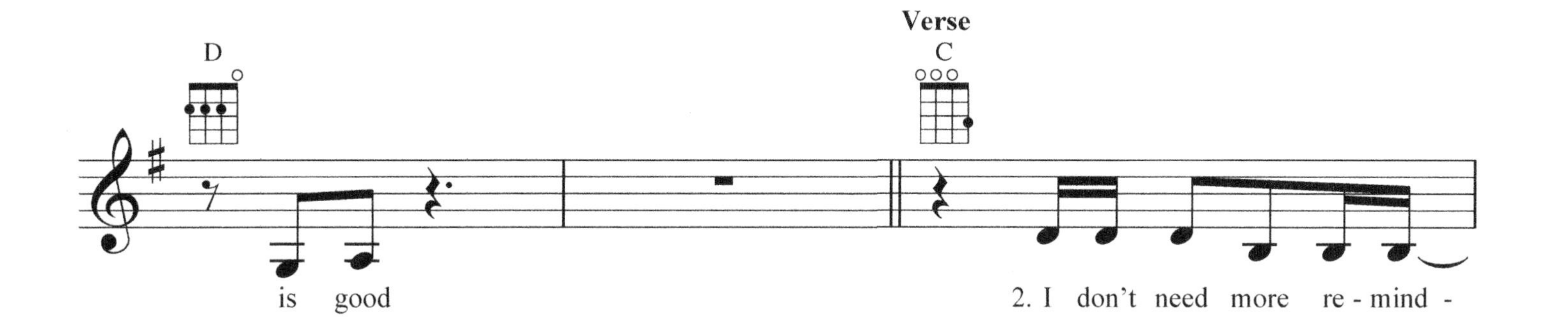
Verse
D
C
is good
2. I don't need more re - mind -

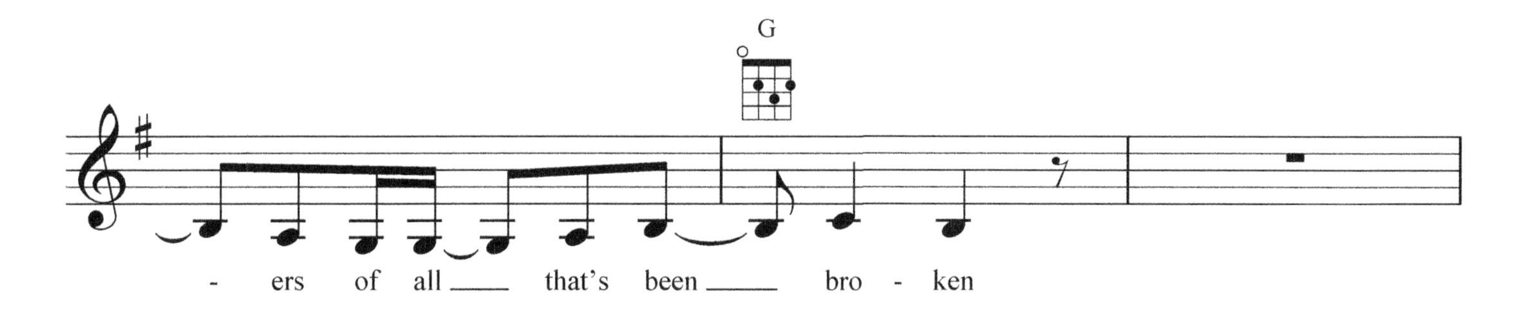
G
- ers of all that's been bro - ken

C
G
I don't need you to fix what I'd rath - er for - get

Em7
Am7
Clear the slate and start o - ver

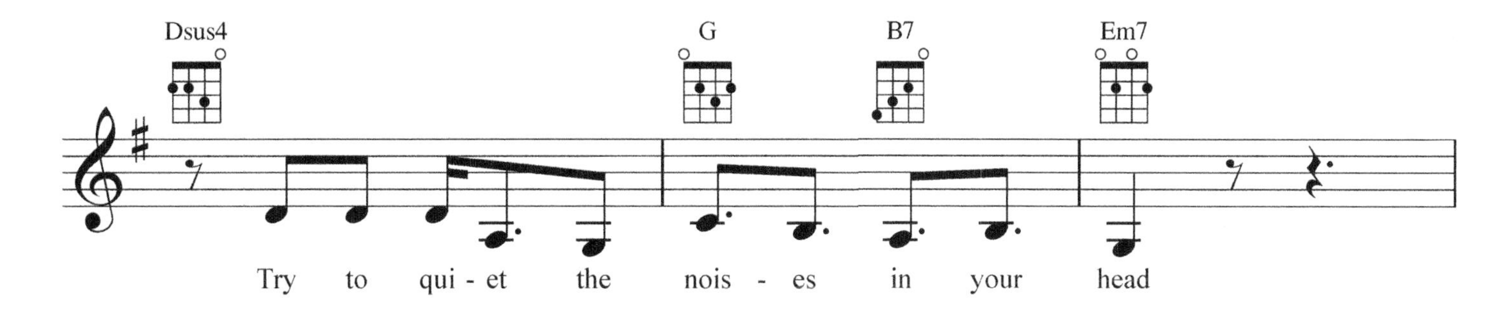
Dsus4
G
B7
Em7
Try to qui - et the nois - es in your head

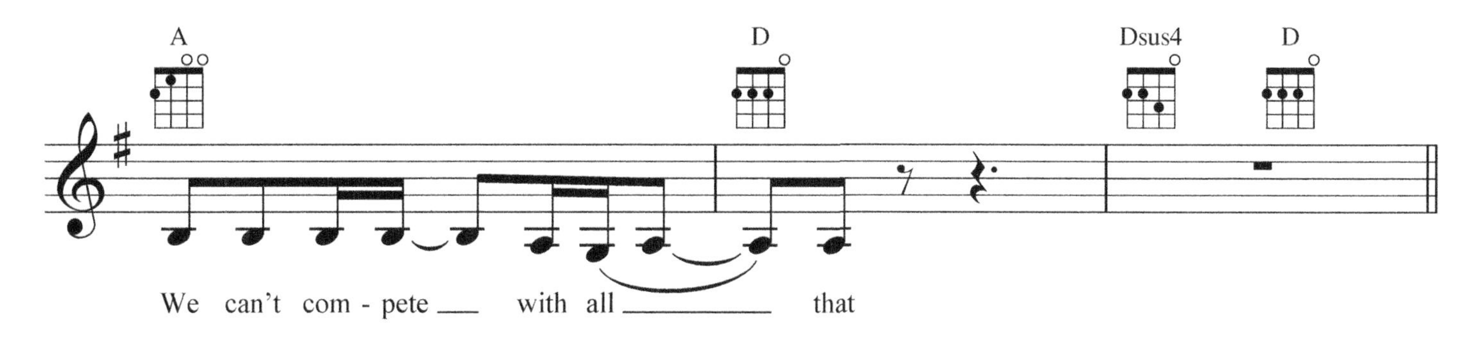
A
D
Dsus4
D
We can't com - pete with all that

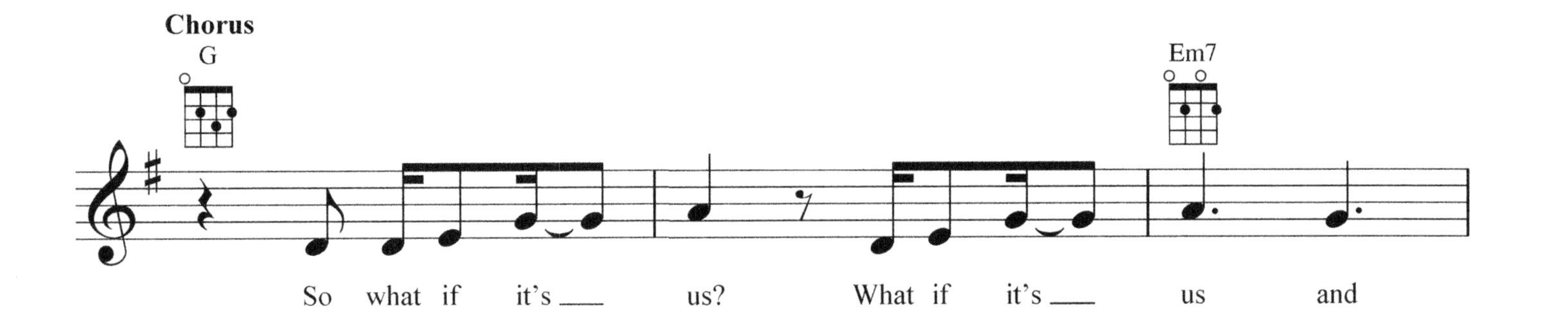
Chorus
G
Em7
So what if it's ___ us? What if it's ___ us and

Am7
on - ly us? And what came be - fore ___ won't count an - y - more, ___

D
G
___ or mat - ter Can we try ___ that? ___ What if it's ___

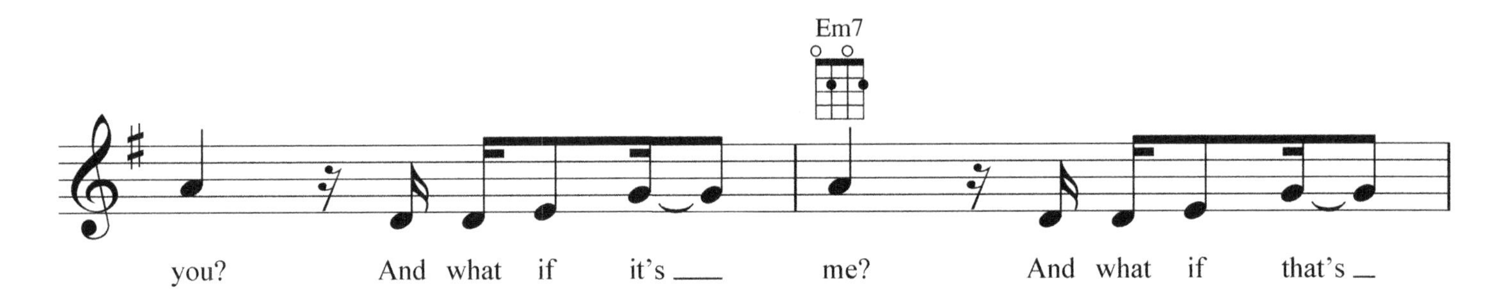
Em7
you? And what if it's ___ me? And what if that's ___

B♭
all that we need it to be? ___ And the rest ___

F
Am7
D
___ of the world ___ falls a - way What do you say?

Verse
G
EVAN: keep conversational throughout
3. I nev - er thought there'd be some - one like you who would
D
Gmaj7
want me
So I give you ten thou - sand
G6
D
rea - sons to not let me go
Bm7
Em7
But if you real - ly see me
A
D
F♯7
If you like me for me and noth - ing
Bm7
E
Asus4
else
Well, that's all that I've want - ed for long - er than you could

Chorus
A7sus4
D
pos - si - bly know
So it can be us It can be

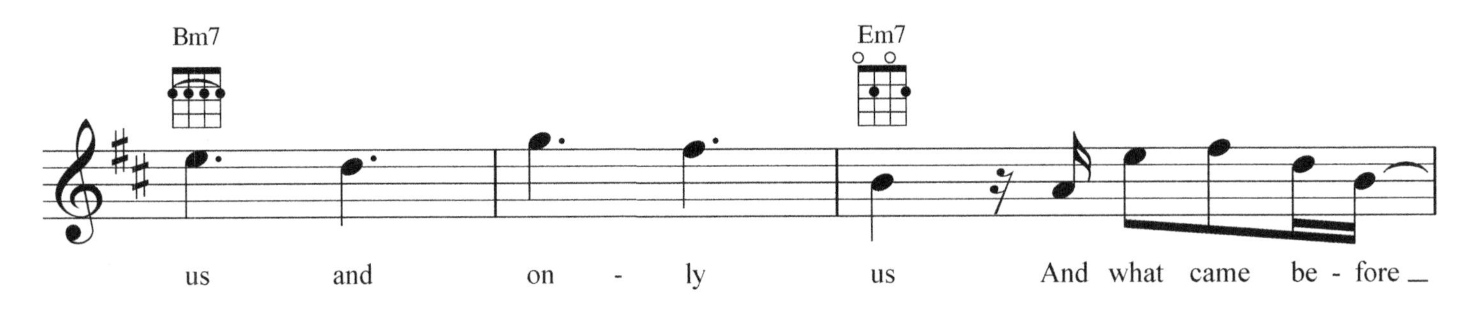
Bm7
Em7
us and on - ly us And what came be - fore

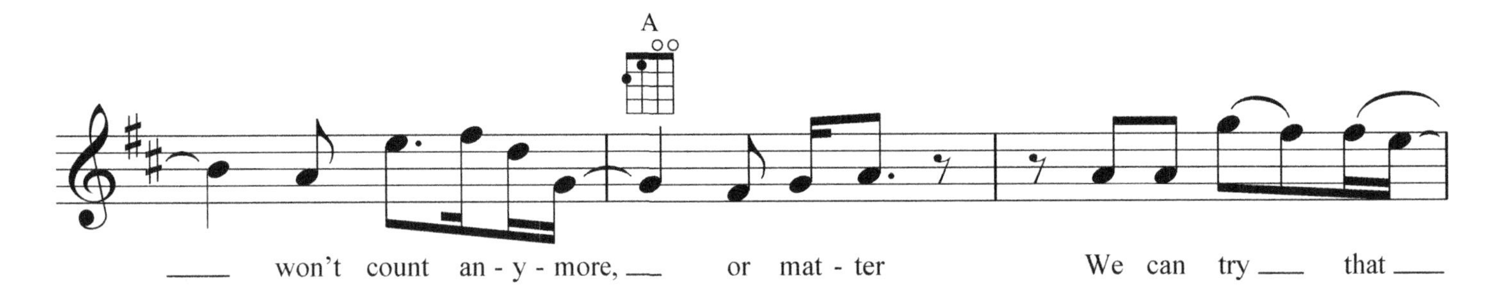
A
won't count an - y - more, or mat - ter We can try that

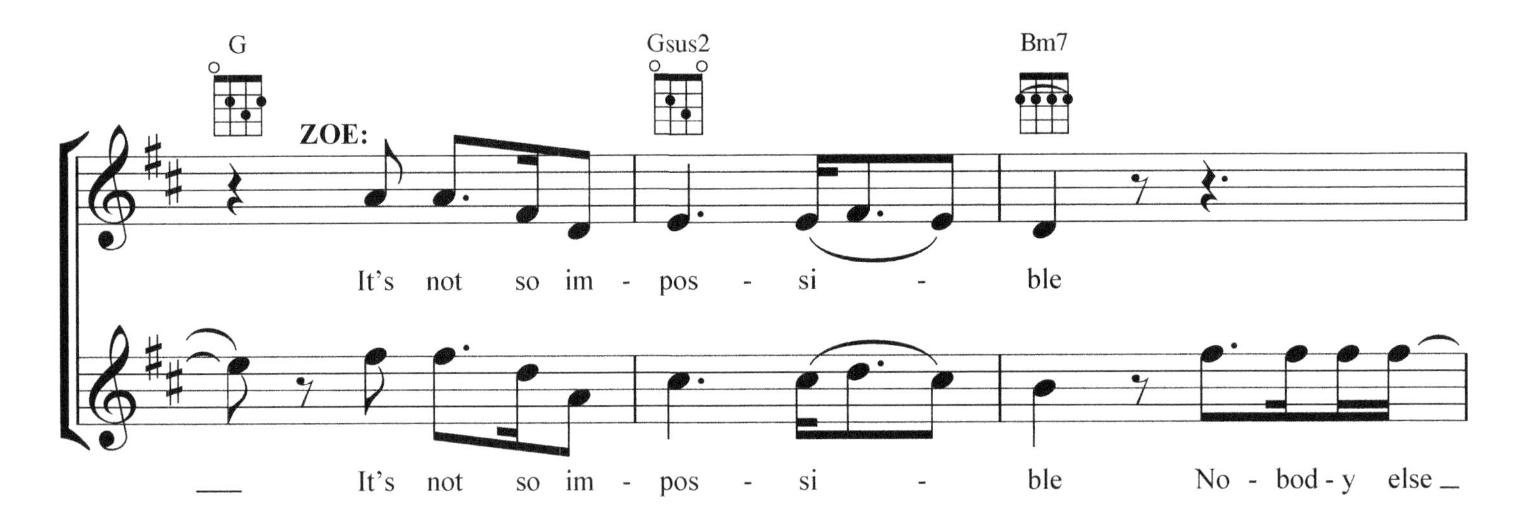
G
Gsus2
Bm7
ZOE:
It's not so im - pos - si - ble
It's not so im - pos - si - ble No - bod - y else

Asus4
A
Gsus2
'Cause you're say - ing it's pos - si -
but the two of us here 'Cause you're say - ing it's pos - si -

Bm7 Asus4 A Gsus2
ble We can just watch the whole world dis - ap - pear 'Til
ble 'Til

Bm7 D A
you're the on - ly one I
you're the on - ly one I

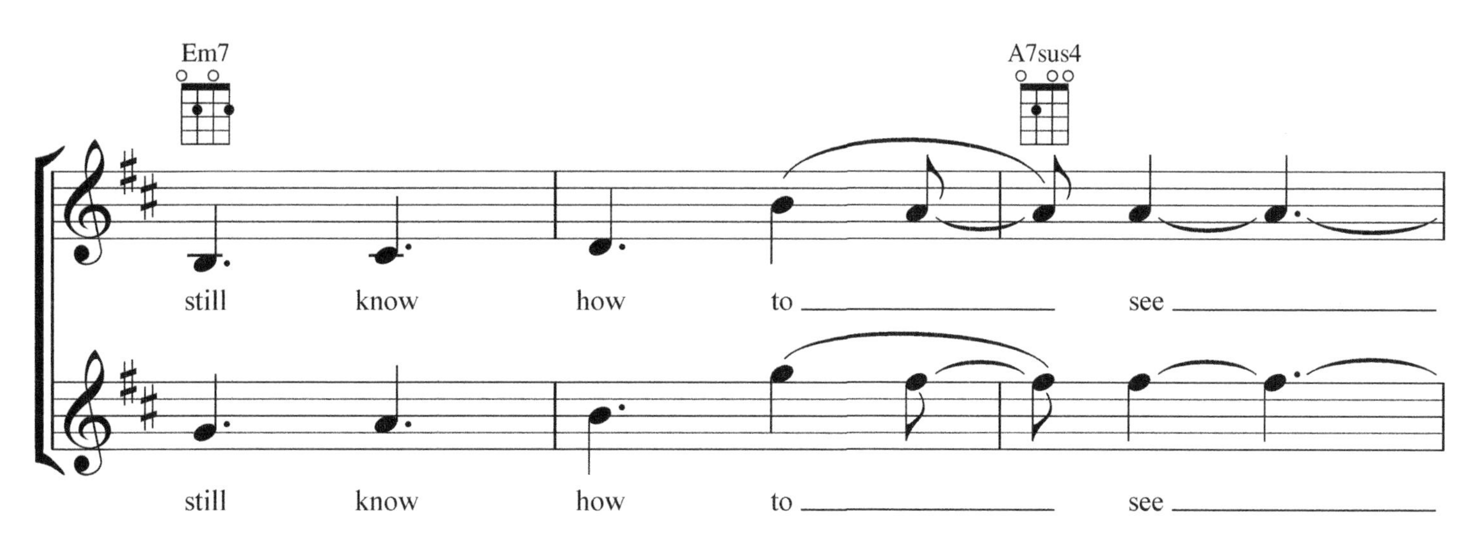
Em7 A7sus4
still know how to see
still know how to see

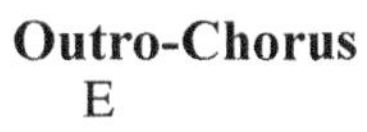
Outro-Chorus

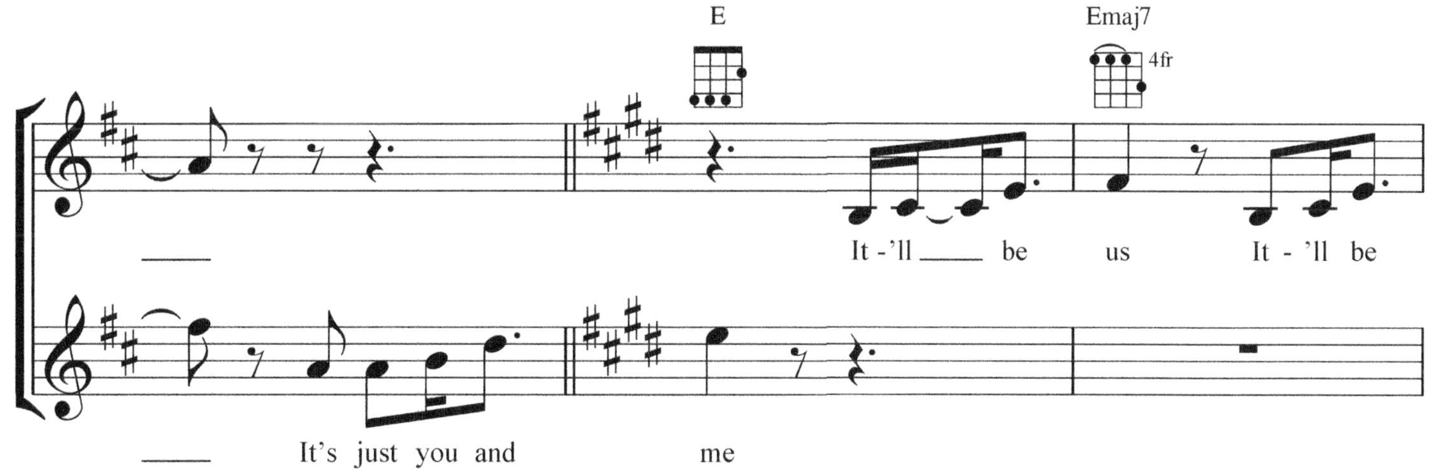
E Emaj7
4fr
It -'ll be us It -'ll be
It's just you and me

C♯m7
F♯m
ZOE:
us and on - ly us And what came be - fore
won't count an - y - more
A
We can try that
EVAN:
We can try that
E
C♯m7
You and me That's
You and me That's
G
D
all that we need it to be And the rest of the world falls a - way
all that we need it to be And the rest of the world falls a - way

C
G
D
F♯m
And the rest of the world falls a - way
And the rest of the world falls a - way
B7sus4
The world falls a - way
The world falls a - way
E
C♯m7
E
C♯m7
The world falls a - way
And it's on - ly
The world falls a - way
And it's on - ly
E
C♯m7
B
A
E
us
us

Good for You

Music and Lyrics by Benj Pasek and Justin Paul

E♭sus2
B♭
Cm7
A♭
3fr
ci - sion
Yeah, I hope it's all that you want and
E♭sus2
Fm
Cm7
more
Now you're free
From the ag - o - niz - ing life
B♭
A♭maj7
Pre-Chorus
Fm
you were liv - ing be - fore
And you say what you need to say
Cm7
Fm
Cm7
So that you get to walk a - way
It would kill you to have to stay trapped
B♭sus4
Fm
when you've got some - thin' new
Well, I'm sor - ry you had it rough

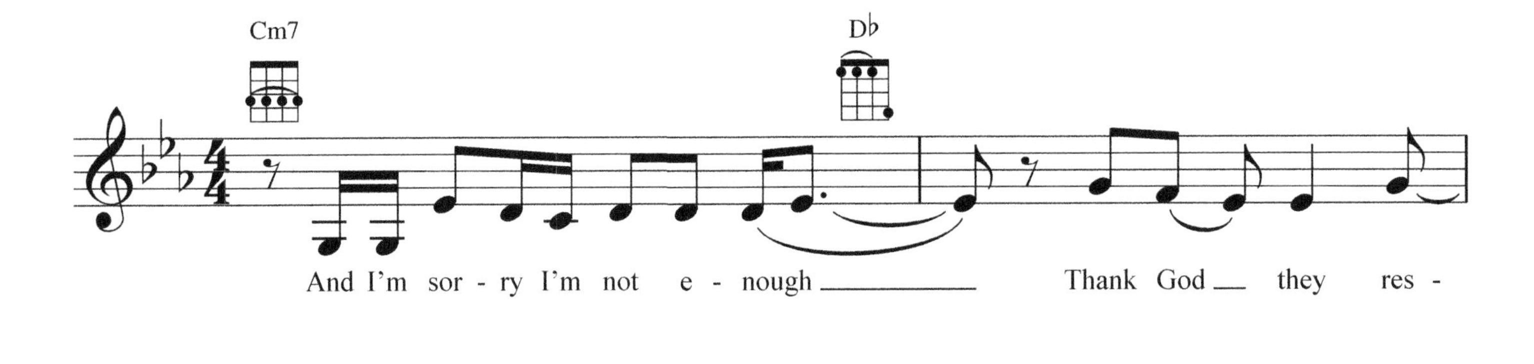
Cm7
D♭
And I'm sor - ry I'm not e - nough
Thank God they res -

Chorus
G
G7
A♭
3fr
E♭sus2
- cued you
So you got what you al - ways want - ed

B♭
Cm7
A♭
3fr
E♭sus2
So you got your dream - come - true
Well, good for you

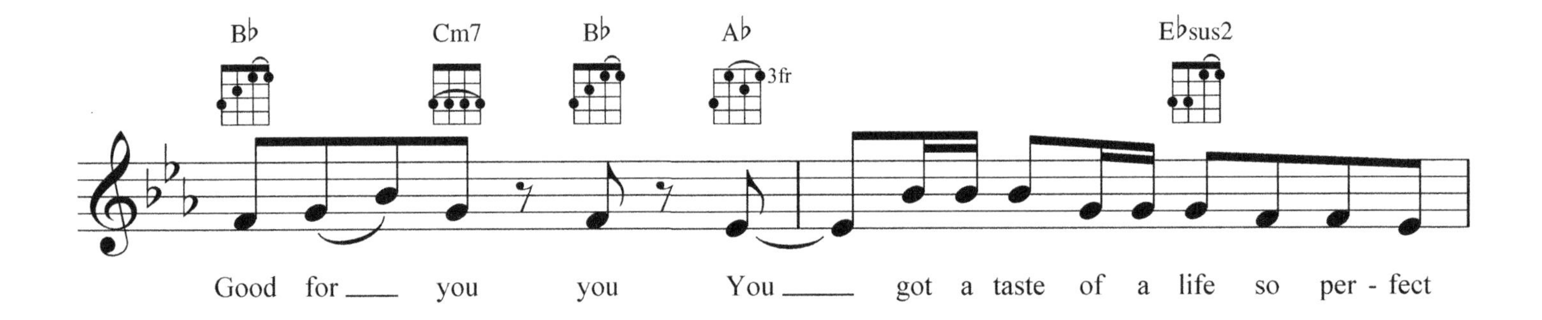
B♭
Cm7
B♭
A♭
3fr
E♭sus2
Good for you you you
You got a taste of a life so per - fect

B♭
Cm7
A♭
3fr
E♭sus2
So you did what you had to do
Good for you

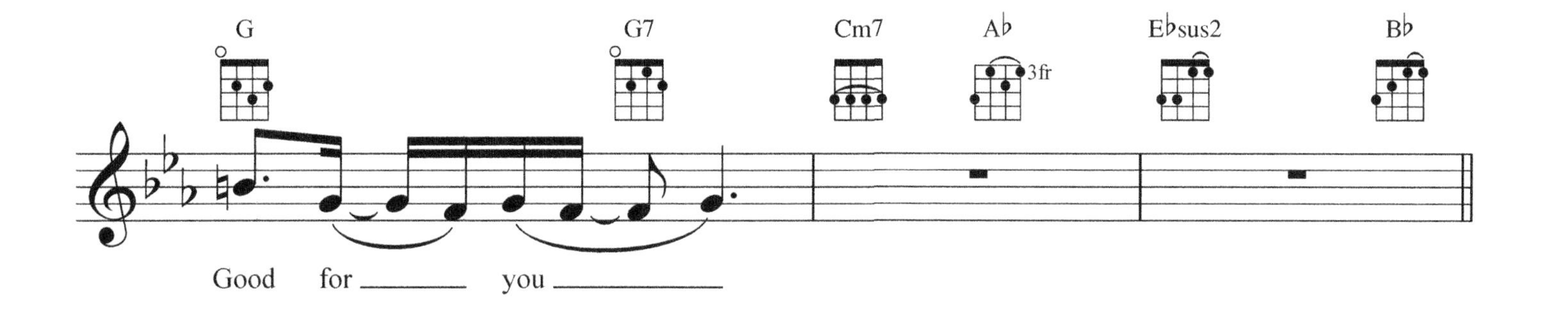
G
G7
Cm7
A♭
3fr
E♭sus2
B♭
Good for you

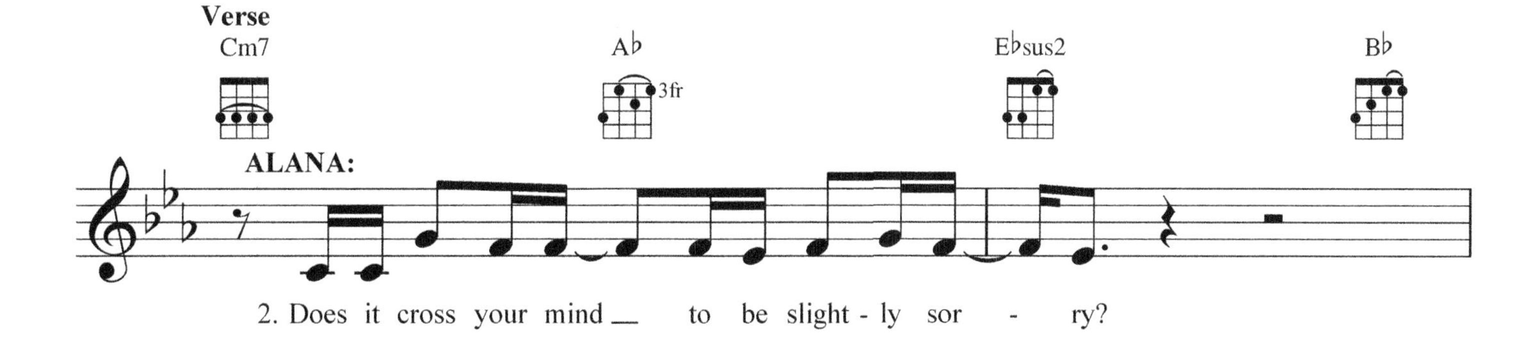
Verse
Cm7
A♭
3fr
E♭sus2
B♭
ALANA:
2. Does it cross your mind to be slight - ly sor - ry?

Cm7
A♭
3fr
E♭sus2
Do you e - ven care that you might be wrong? Was it fun?

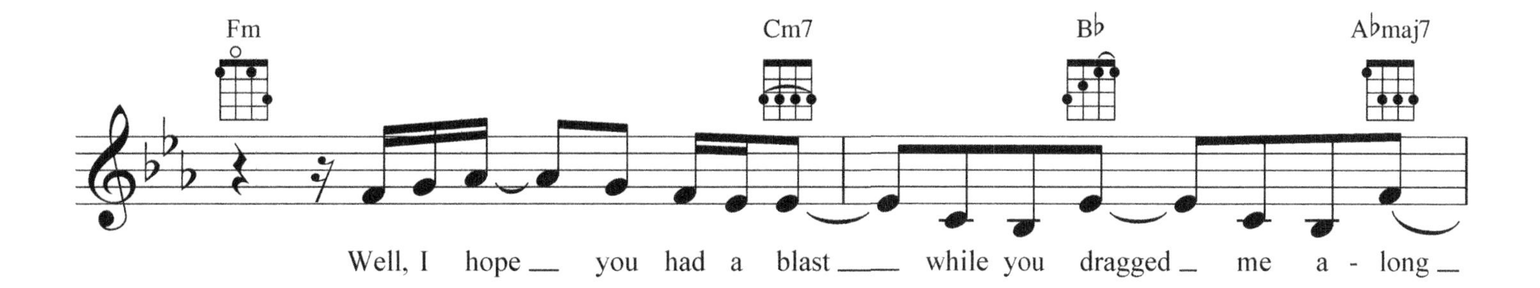
Fm
Cm7
B♭
A♭maj7
Well, I hope you had a blast while you dragged me a - long

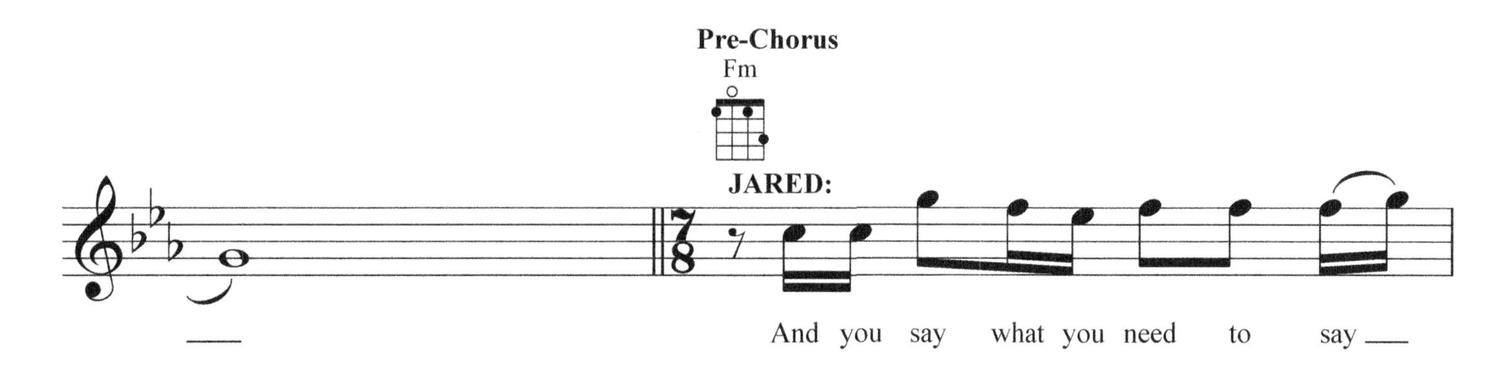
Pre-Chorus
Fm
JARED:
And you say what you need to say

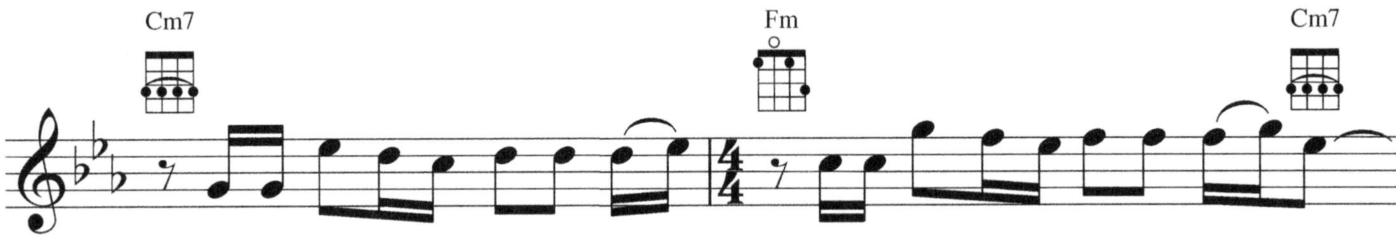
Cm7
Fm
Cm7
And you play who you need to play
And if some-bod-y's in your way, crush

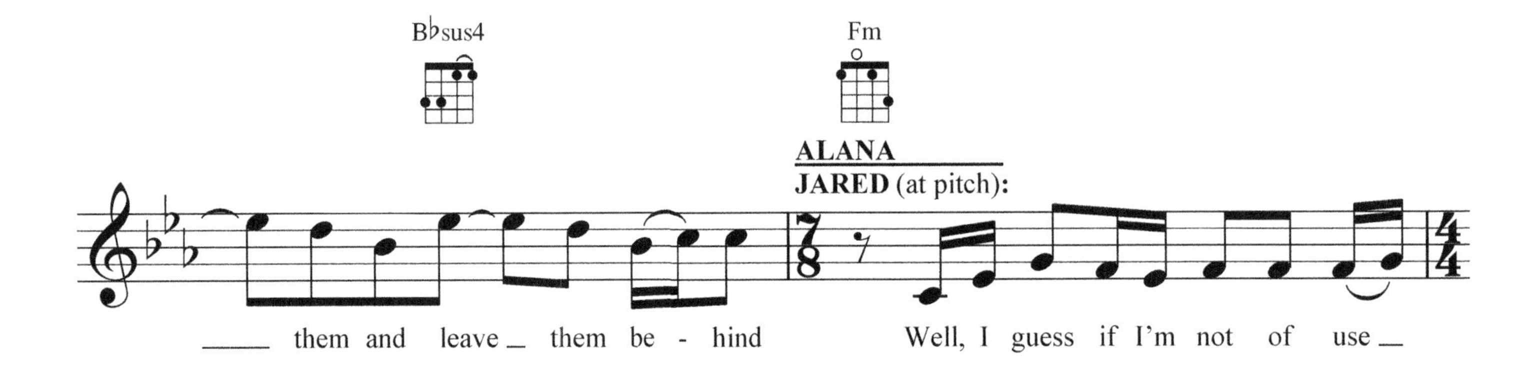
B♭sus4
Fm
ALANA
JARED (at pitch):
them and leave them be-hind
Well, I guess if I'm not of use

Cm7
D♭
Go a-head you can cut me loose
Go a-head now I

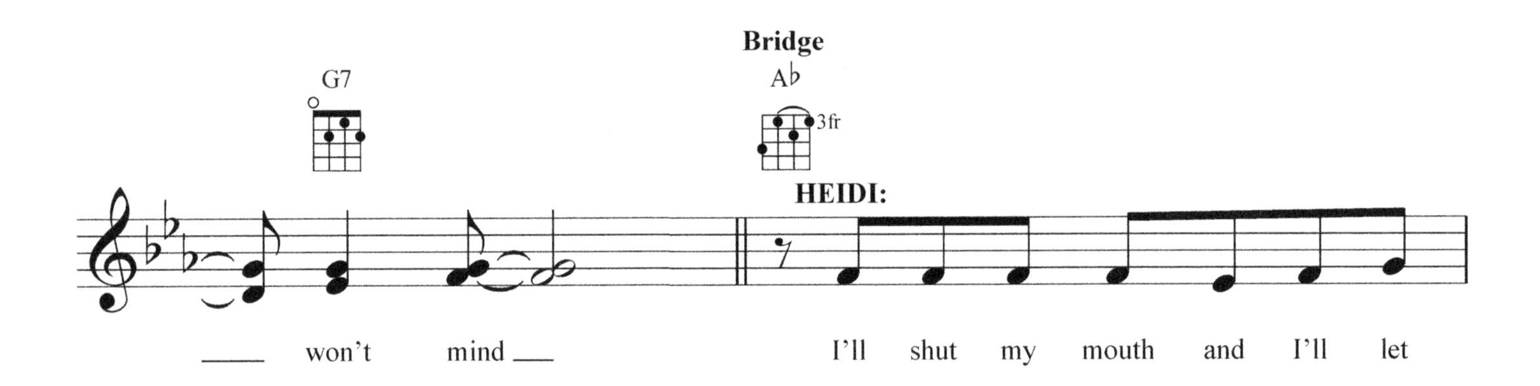
Bridge
G7
A♭
3fr
HEIDI:
won't mind
I'll shut my mouth and I'll let

E♭sus2
B♭
you go
Is that good for you?
Would that be

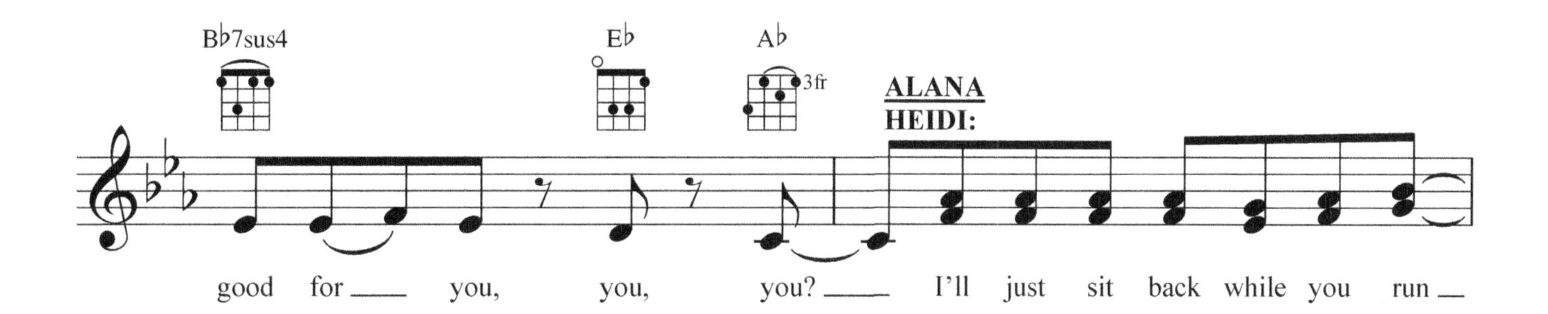

B♭7sus4
E♭
A♭
3fr
ALANA
HEIDI:
good for ___ you, you, you? ___ I'll just sit back while you run ___

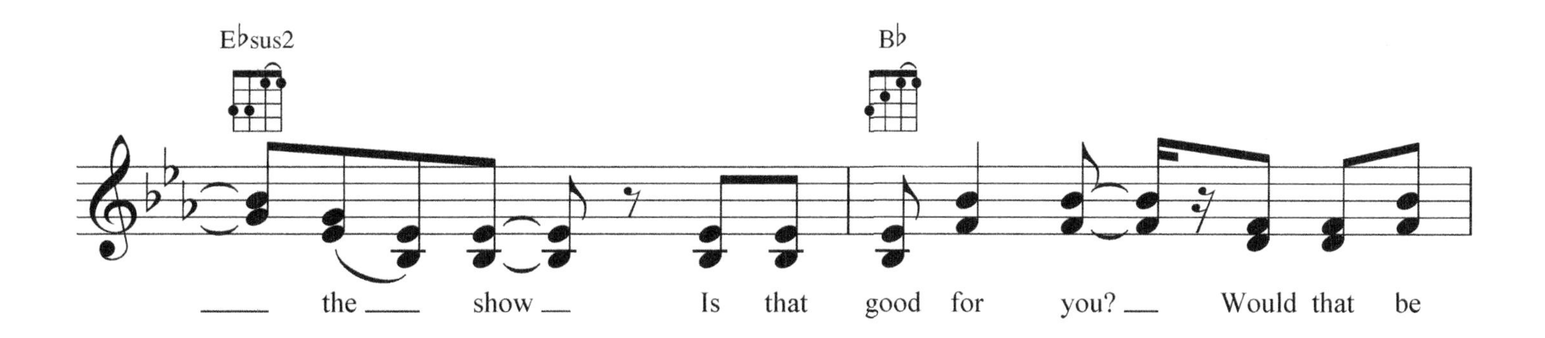

E♭sus2
B♭
___ the ___ show ___ Is that good for you? ___ Would that be

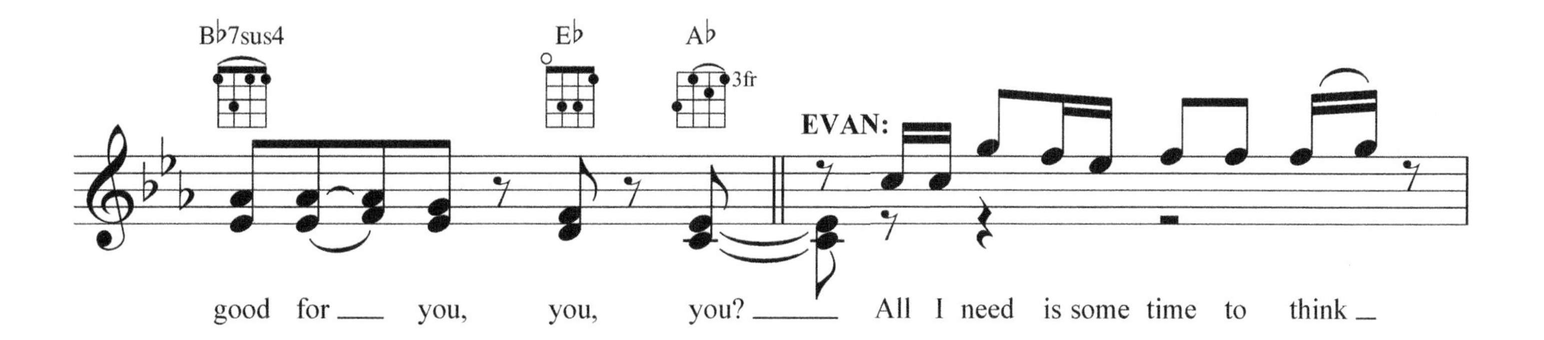

B♭7sus4
E♭
A♭
3fr
EVAN:
good for ___ you, you, you? ___ All I need is some time to think ___

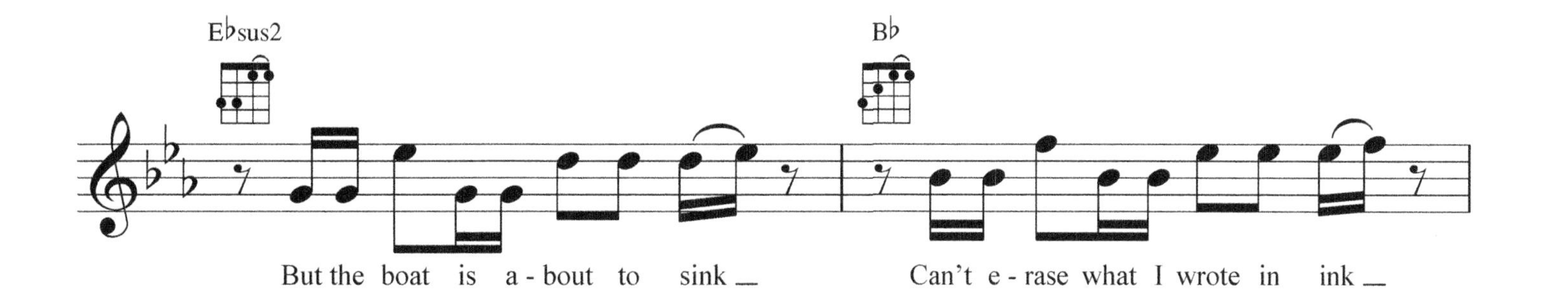

E♭sus2
B♭
But the boat is a - bout to sink ___ Can't e - rase what I wrote in ink ___

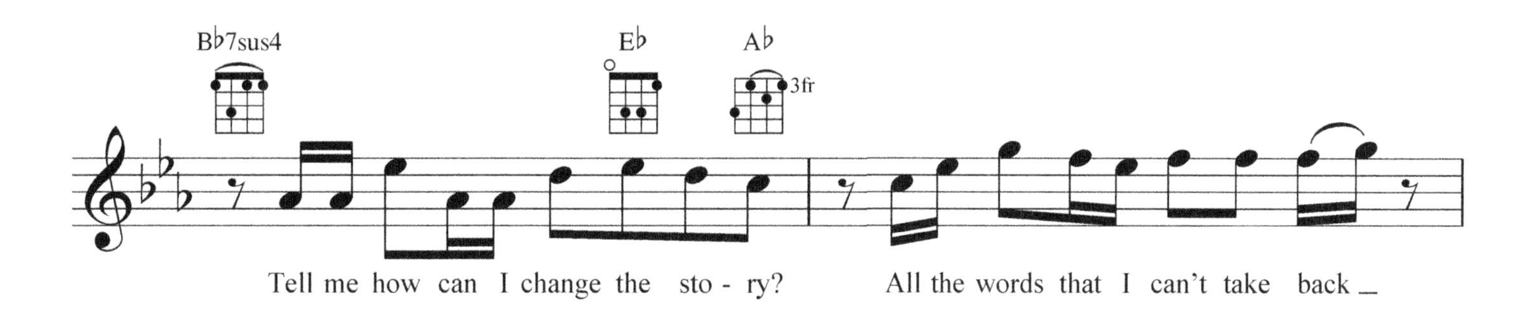

B♭7sus4
E♭
A♭
3fr
Tell me how can I change the sto - ry? All the words that I can't take back ___

E♭sus2
Fm
Like a train com - in' off the track
As the rails and the bolts all crack
G7
B♭
I got - ta find a way to Stop it Stop it Just let me out
F
C
Dm7
ALANA
HEIDI:
So you got what you al - ways want - ed So you got your dream - come - true
JARED:
B♭
F
C
Dm
C
B♭
ALANA
HEIDI:
good for you Good for you you You
JARED
EVAN:

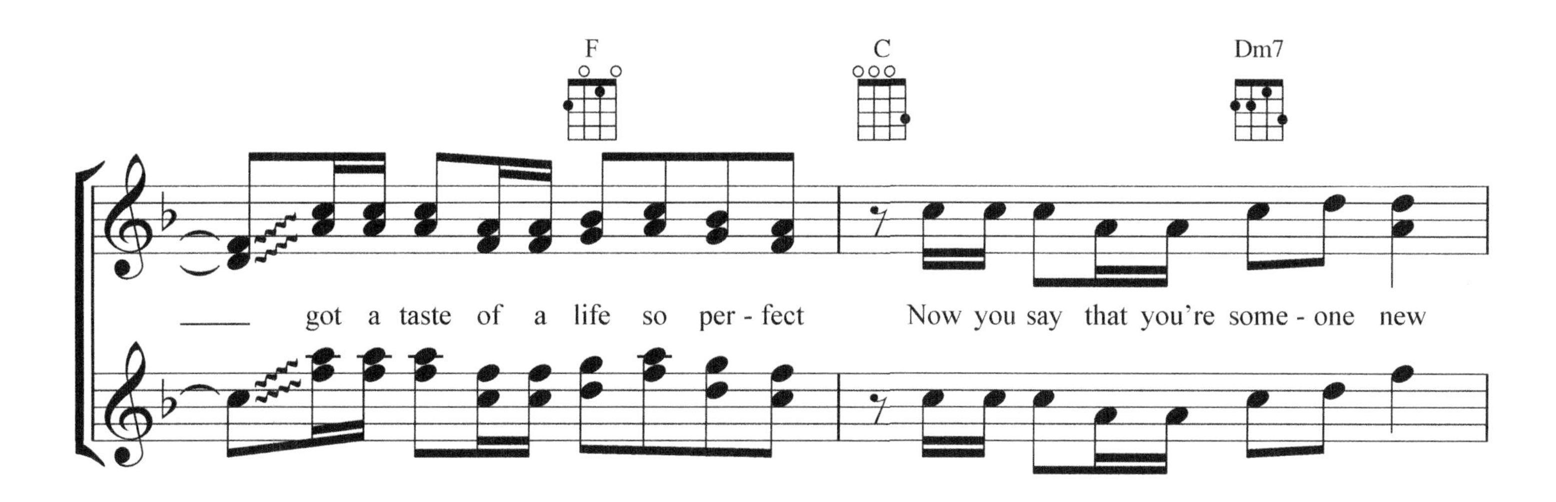
F
C
Dm7
got a taste of a life so per - fect
Now you say that you're some - one new

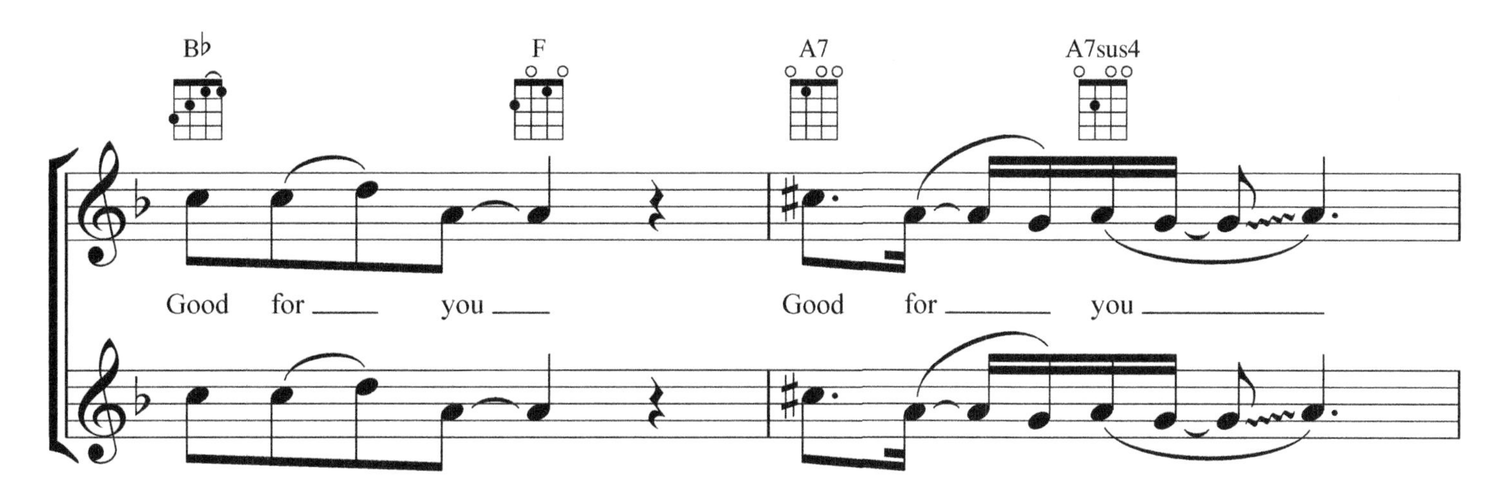
B♭
F
A7
A7sus4
Good for you
Good for you

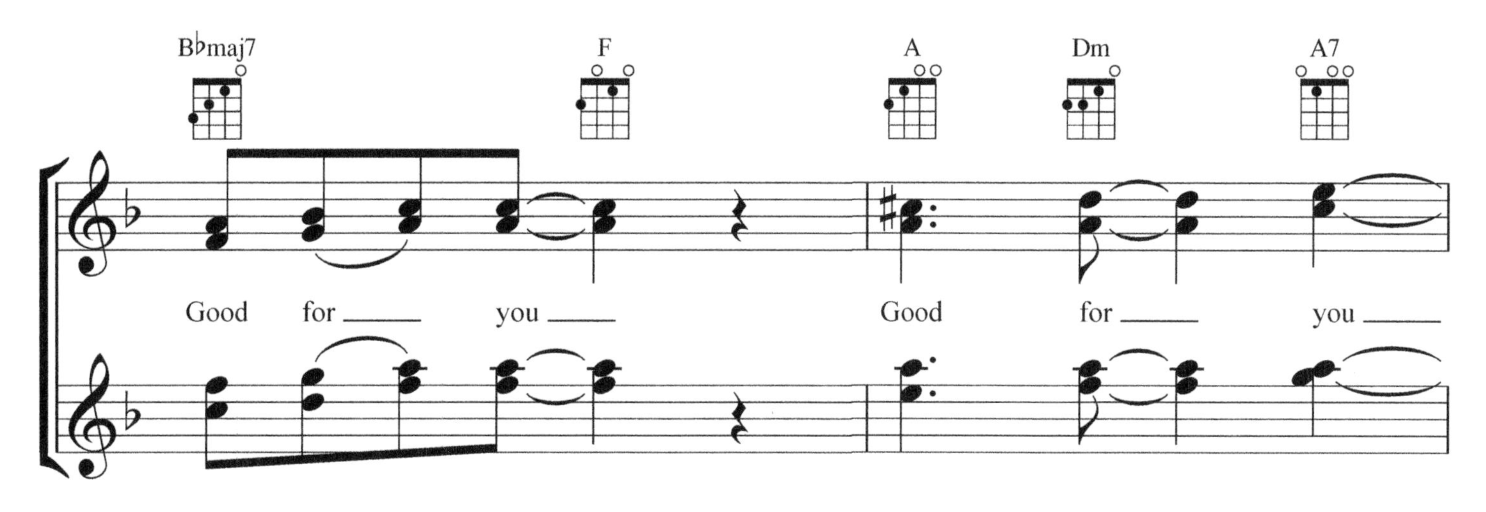
B♭maj7
F
A
Dm
A7
Good for you
Good for you

B♭
N.C.
D
ALANA/HEIDI:
So you got what you al - ways want - ed
JARED:

Words Fail

Music and Lyrics by Benj Pasek and Justin Paul

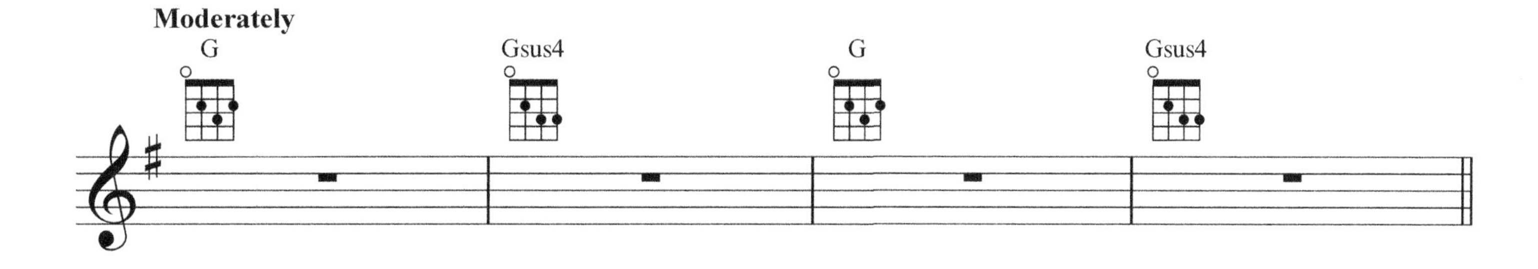
Moderately
G
Gsus4
G
Gsus4

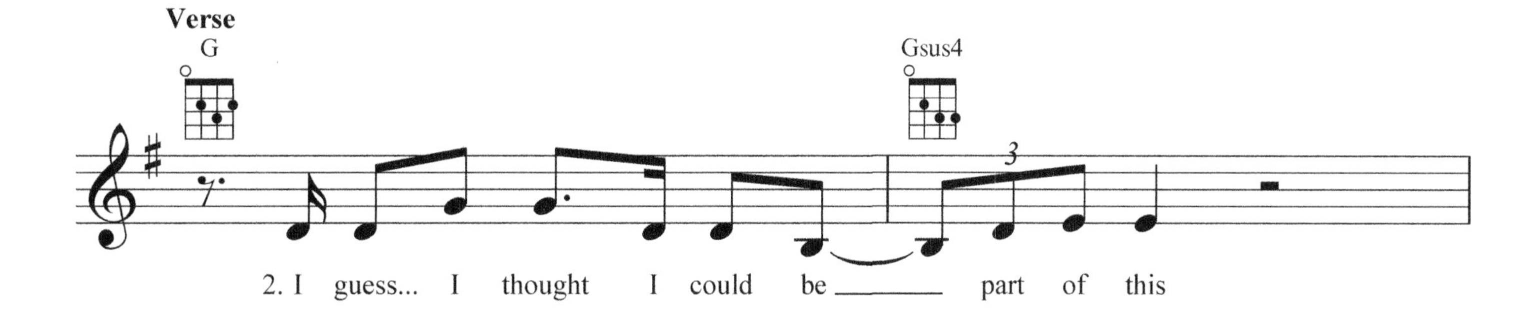
Verse
G
Gsus4
2. I guess... I thought I could be part of this

G
Gsus4
I nev - er had this kind of thing be - fore

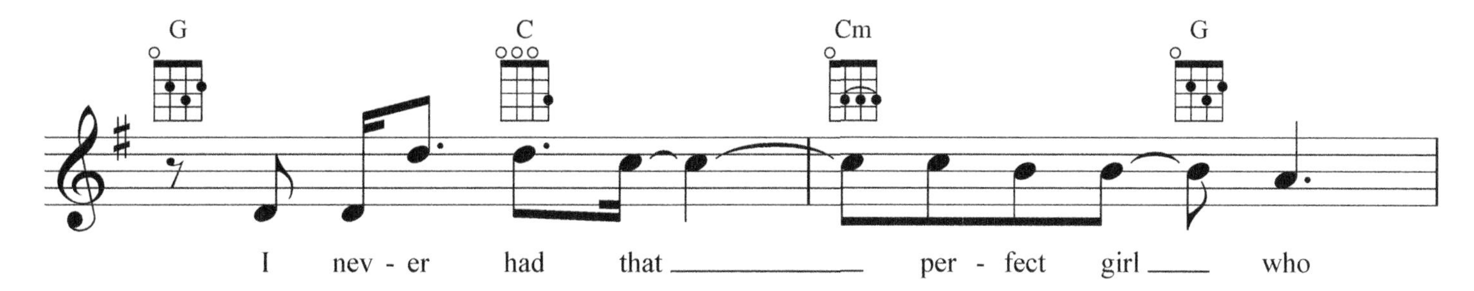
G
C
Cm
G
I nev - er had that per - fect girl who

A7
C
some - how could see the good part of me

Verse
G
Gsus4
3. I nev - er had the dad who stuck it out

G
Gsus4
No corn - y jokes or base - ball gloves
G
C
Cm
G
A7
No mom who just was there 'cause "Mom" was all that she had
Pre-Chorus
D
Em
C
to be
That's not a wor - thy ex - pla - na - tion
G
Dsus2
Em
3
3
3
I know there is none
Noth - ing can make sense
Slower
Bm
Am
D
Am
D
Am7
Gmaj7
of all these things I've done
Words
Chorus
C
D
G
C
Fsus2
3
3
fail
Words fail
There's noth - ing I can say

Pushing, with intensity
G
C
ex - cept, some - times you see ev - 'ry - thing you've want - ed and
Fsus2
G
C
some - times you see ev - 'ry - thing you wish you had and it's
Fsus2
G
Am7
G
right there, right there, right there in
Rubato, sempre colla voce
C
Fadd9
front of you And you want to be -
C
Fadd9
C
Fsus2
lieve it's true So you make it true And you think
Am7
C
Fsus2
Cmaj7
may - be ev - 'ry - bod - y wants it, needs it a lit - tle bit

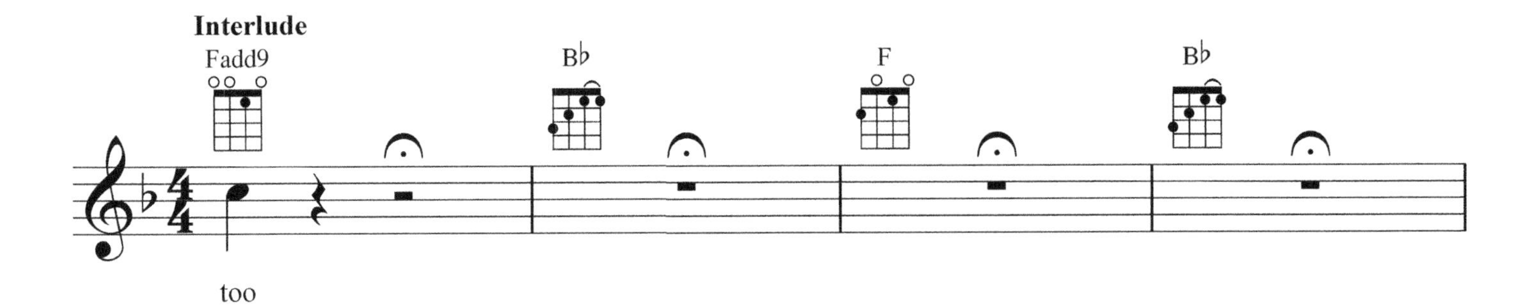
Interlude
Fadd9
B♭
F
B♭
too

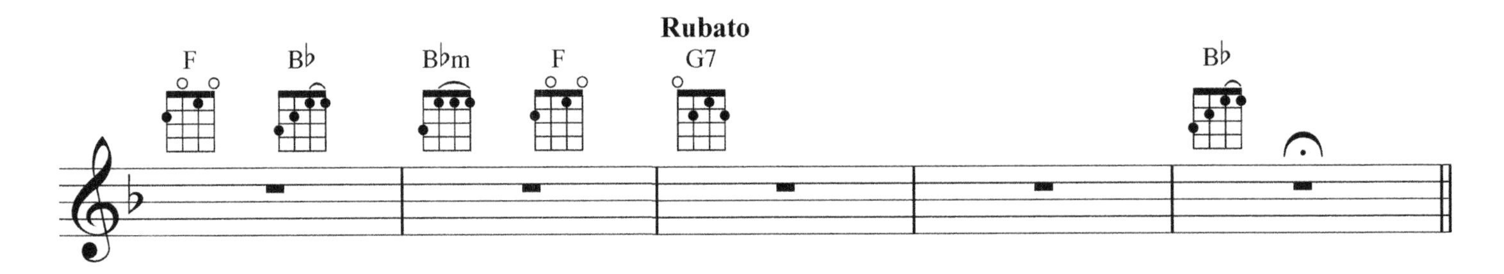
F
B♭
B♭m
F
Rubato
G7
B♭

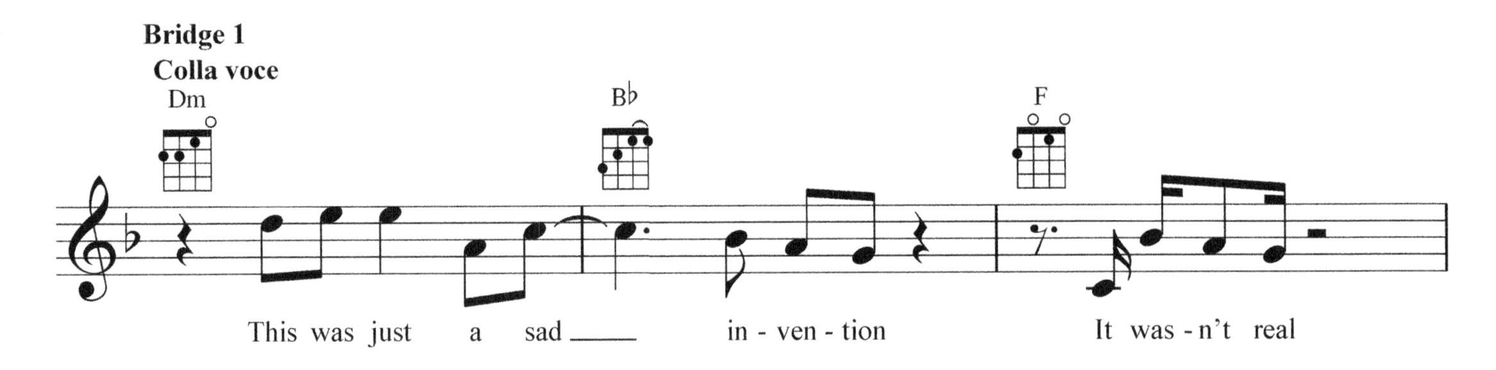
Bridge 1
Colla voce
Dm
B♭
F
This was just a sad in - ven - tion
It was - n't real

Dm
Am
I know
But we were hap - py
I guess I could - n't

Moderately
B♭
F
3
let that go
I guess I could - n't
give that up

Dm7
I guess I want - ed to be - lieve
'Cause if I just be - lieve

C
Bb
then I don't have to see what's real - ly there
A little faster
Dm7
No, I'd rath - er pre - tend I'm some - thing bet - ter than these
Bb
F
bro - ken parts Pre - tend I'm some - thing oth - er than this
C
Dm7
mess that I am 'Cause then I don't have to look at it and
Bb
F
Bb
C
no one gets to look at it No, no one can real - ly see
Bridge 2
With fervor
Am7
Fadd9
Gsus4
'Cause I've learned to slam on the brake

C
Fadd9
Gsus4
Am7
Fadd9
Be - fore I e - ven turn the key
Be - fore I make
Gsus4
C
Fadd9
the mis - take
Be - fore I lead with the worst
Am7
Gsus4
C
Fsus2
of me
I nev - er let them see the worst
Outro
A tempo
Am
G
C
of me
Fsus2
'Cause what if ev - 'ry - one saw?
What if ev - 'ry - one knew?
C
Fsus2
Would they like what they saw?
Or would they

Am7 Gsus4 Dm7 Am7 G C
hate it too? Will I just keep on run - ning a - way
Rubato, colla voce
Fadd9 Am Fsus2
from what's true? All I ev - er do is run
G Dm7 Fsus2
So how do I step in, step in - to the sun?
Moderately
C Dm7(add4) Fsus2 C Dm7(add4) Fsus2
Step in - to the sun
C Dm7(add4) Fsus2 C Dm7(add4) Fsus2
C Dm7(add4) Fsus2 C Dm7(add4) Fadd9

So Big/So Small

Music and Lyrics by Benj Pasek and Justin Paul

Dsus4
D
Em7
D
Am7
smiled so wide A real live truck in your drive-way
Pre-Chorus
Dsus4
D
G
C
D
We let you sit be-hind the wheel Good-bye
G
C
G
good-bye Now it's just me and my
Chorus
Em7
Fsus2
Dm7(add4)
C
G
lit-tle guy And the house felt so big And I
Dm7(add4)
C
G
Dm7(add4)
C
felt so small The house felt so
G
Dm7(add4)
C
G
big And I felt so small

Verse
G C Dsus4 D G C
3. That night I tucked you in to bed I will nev-er for-get how you
Dsus4 D Em7 D
sat up and said "Is there an - oth-er truck com-in' to our
Am7 Dsus4 D G
drive-way A truck that will take Mom-my a-way?" And the house
Chorus
G7sus4 C G G7sus4 C G
felt so big And I felt so small The house
G7sus4 C G Dm7(add4)
felt so big And I And I
Bridge
Moving forward (still rubato)
C Em D
knew there would be mo - ments that I'd miss And

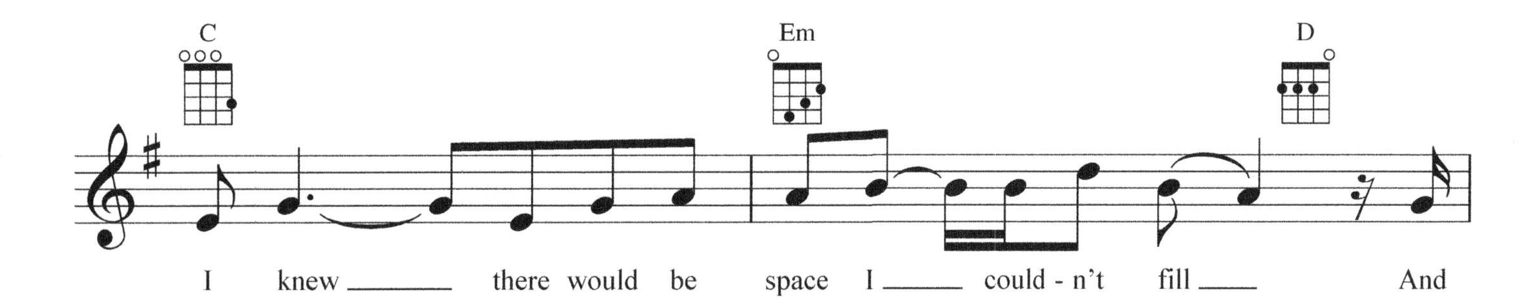
C
Em
D
I knew there would be space I could - n't fill And

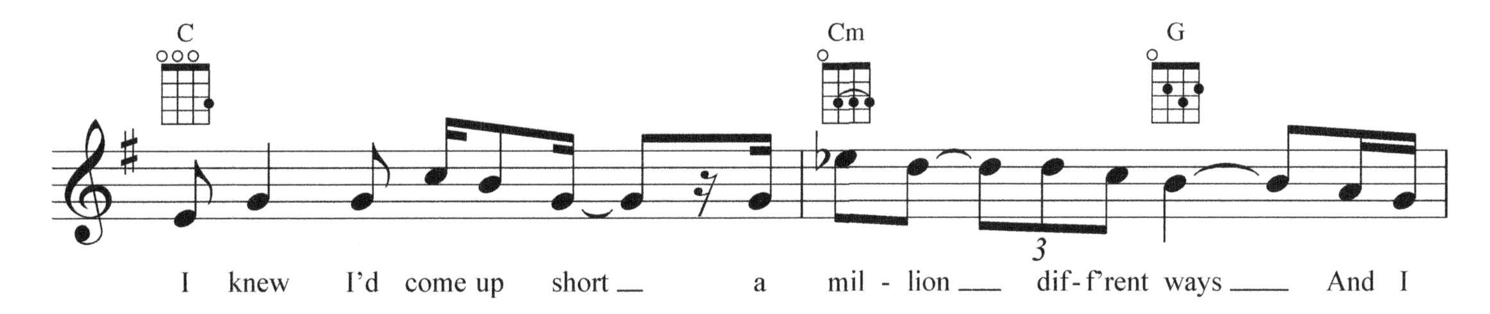
C
Cm
G
3
I knew I'd come up short a mil - lion dif - f'rent ways And I

Colla voce
Dsus4
C
D
did, and I do, and I will

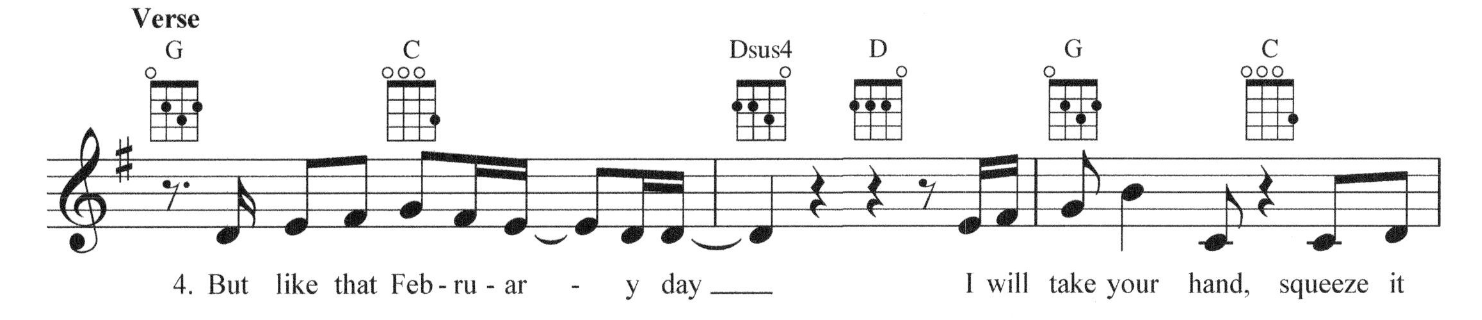
Verse
G
C
Dsus4
D
G
C
4. But like that Feb - ru - ar - y day I will take your hand, squeeze it

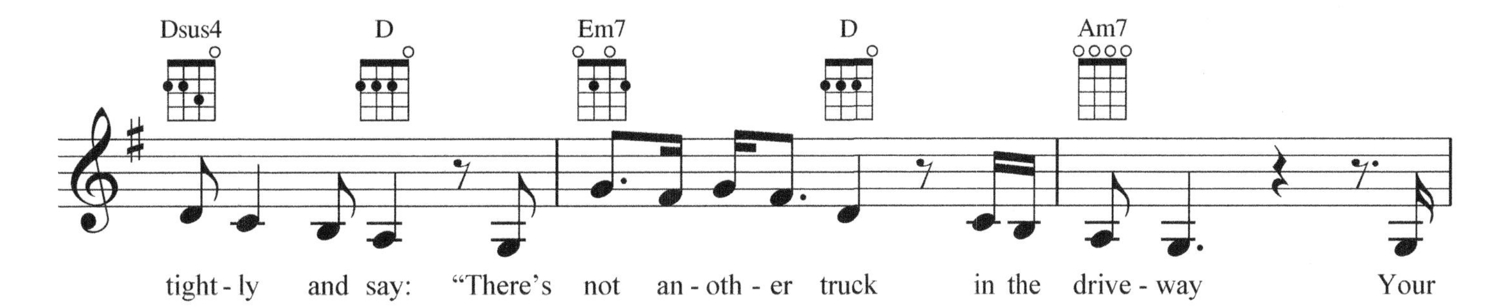
Dsus4
D
Em7
D
Am7
tight - ly and say: "There's not an - oth - er truck in the drive - way Your

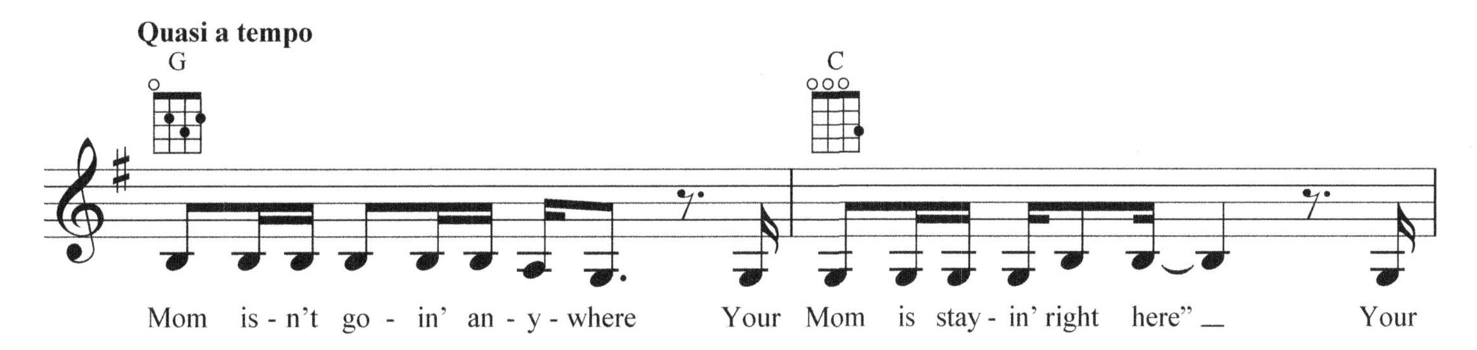
Quasi a tempo
G
C
Mom is - n't go - in' an - y - where Your Mom is stay - in' right here" Your

Dsus4
B7
Mom is-n't go-in' an-y-where Your Mom is stay-in' right here No mat-ter
Slowly
Em
G
Outro-Chorus
Quasi a tempo
G7sus4
C
what I'll be here when it all feels so
G
G7sus4
C
G
big 'Til it all feels so small When it
Dm7(add4)
C
G
Dm7(add4)
C
all feels so big 'Til it all feels so
Em
A
Colla voce
Dsus4
D
As before
G
C
small 'Til it all feels so small
Dsus4
D
G
C
Dsus4
D
G